NEBRASKA ~~WNCC Library~~

NO LONGER PROPERTY OF

GN
273

D0915867

HUMAN DEVELOPMENT BOOKS:
A SERIES IN APPLIED BEHAVIORAL SCIENCE

Joseph and Laurie Braga, *general editors*

HUMAN DEVELOPMENT BOOKS is a series designed to bridge the gap between theory and research in the behavioral sciences and practical application by readers. Each book in the series deals with an issue important to the growth and development of human beings, as individuals and in interaction with one another. At a time when the pressures and complexities of the world are making increased demands on people's ability to cope, there is a need for tools that can help individuals take a more active role in solving their own problems and in living life more fully. Such information is not easily found or read by those without previous experience or familiarity with the vocabulary of a particular behavioral field. The books in this series were designed and executed to meet that purpose.

ASHLEY MONTAGU is a world-famous anthropologist and social biologist. He is the author of numerous books, including *The Direction of Human Development: Biological and Social Bases of Love; On Being Human; Prenatal Influences; Touching; Sex, Man, and Society;* and *The Practice of Love* (Prentice-Hall, 1974).

BOOKS IN THE SERIES

Growing with Children, by Joseph and Laurie Braga
Growing Older, by Margaret Hellie Huyck
Learning and Growing: A Guide to Child Development,
by Laurie and Joseph Braga
Culture and Human Development: Insights into Growing Human,
by Ashley Montagu
Death: The Final Stage of Growth, by Elisabeth Kübler-Ross
(in production)

CULTURE
AND
HUMAN
DEVELOPMENT

Insights into
Growing Human

Edited by

Ashley Montagu

PRENTICE-HALL, INC. Englewood Cliffs, N. J.
A SPECTRUM BOOK

NEBRASKA WESTERN COLLEGE
LIBRARY

Library of Congress Cataloging in Publication Data

MONTAGU, ASHLEY, comp.
Culture and human development; insights into growing human.

(Human development books)   (A Spectrum Book)
Includes bibliographies.
    1. Ethnopsychology.   2. Personality and culture.
3. Children—Growth.   4. Environmental psychology.
I. Title.
GN273.M66   301.2   74–18338
ISBN 0–13–195578–0
ISBN 0–13–195560–8 (pbk.)

© 1974 by Ashley Montagu.
A SPECTRUM BOOK. All rights reserved. No part of this
book may be reproduced in any form or by any means without
permission in writing from the publisher. Printed in the United
States of America.

10 9 8 7 6 5 4 3 2 1

PRENTICE-HALL INTERNATIONAL, INC. (*London*)

PRENTICE-HALL OF AUSTRALIA PTY. LTD. (*Sydney*)

PRENTICE-HALL OF CANADA LTD. (*Toronto*)

PRENTICE-HALL OF INDIA PRIVATE LIMITED (*New Delhi*)

PRENTICE-HALL OF JAPAN, INC. (*Tokyo*)

CONTENTS

7 & 8

9

10

11

12

13

Foreword

What do you consider to be the most significant influence on your growth as a human being? Why do you think people of different ethnic groups have different behavioral characteristics? Would you believe that a child could be mentally retarded and physically dwarfed because of environmental influences? Do you think that a human baby can be raised by a wolf? Can you imagine any parallel between baby kangaroos and human infants? What do you think is the most serious possible effect of emotional deprivation on children's development? Can you see any connection among these questions?

In this book, Dr. Montagu, through his own writing and selections by others, offers evidence to answer the questions posed above and provoke many more. He presents some startling examples of the ways in which the cultural environment can influence the development of human beings. He challenges, through classic and recent studies, many treasured assumptions, fallacies, and misinterpretations about the human condition and what makes it what it is. Through looking at the sometimes bizarre impacts upon children of inhuman and inhumane environments, Dr. Montagu eloquently leads us to see how humankind's cultures are instrumental in or, conversely, detrimental to the raising of human beings.

If you are like most people, it is likely that you give at least occasional thought to what factors influence the particular capacities that you do or do not have. You probably wonder why you are the way you are, what makes you similar to and different from others. In searching for answers to these kinds of questions, there are some who would like to find clearcut answers, e.g., "You are what you are because of what you inherit from your parents"; "You will be whatever you learn to be—what you are is a function of the environment you grow up in"; "You are the way you are because of the ethnic group to which you belong"; "You share the characteristics of others born under your astrological sign"; and so on. In fact, each individual is like every other in that they are all human beings and share a common human heredity, and each individual is different from any other in that he/she has a unique individual heredity and complex of environmental experiences in which those potentialities may be expressed.

As Dr. Montagu points out in his Introduction, heredity is *not* something you inherit; your genes influence the expression of physical and behavioral characteristics, but it is the cultural environment in which you grow which greatly influences the manner in which those characteristics will be expressed. The "nature–nurture" or heredity vs. environment controversy has been around for a long time, with proponents of each side lining up against each other. The fact is that it is a false distinction and therefore an empty argument. Heredity and environment are not really separable; trying to study either's influence alone is like studying hydrogen and oxygen separately in order to understand the properties of water. It is the interaction of the elements that makes the final substance.

The purpose of this book, therefore, is not to present arguments for the side of environment in making human beings what they are. Rather, it is to focus on some of the more dramatic influences of the cultural milieu in which humans grow, creating consequences that have always been considered a function of biological and genetic determinants. For example, there are several articles included in the volume that illustrate the adverse physical effects upon children of impoverished emotional environments. This is not to say that every child living in an emotionally chilled, inconsistent, and/or unresponsive environment will become mentally retarded or physically dwarfed; clearly they will not. But it is essential that we understand how great an impact the environment has on children's development.

It has been demonstrated (Chess, Thomas, and Birch, 1965; Murphy, 1962) * that children are born with different abilities to cope, to withstand pressures and obstacles to their growth and development. Many children are able to cope with a great deal of anxiety, inconsistent treatment, etc., without its affecting them in any obvious way. Other children seem to fall apart under a great deal of stress. These children, such as those described in the article "Emotional Deprivation and Growth Retardation Simulating Idiopathic Hypopituitarism," should serve to alert us to the impact the emotional environment can potentially have on children's growth. Other children are more likely to be affected in more subtle, less obvious and dramatic ways. This should not be used to reassure us that the effects of the environment are really minor. Rather, we must take the message communicated so dramatically by some children's response to stressful situations as a clue to the perhaps more subtle impact these and less obviously detrimental environments are having on a much larger population of children. Any aspect of treatment of children which reduces their growth potential must be of concern to all of us. Children are the only promise for the future of the human race; we cannot allow their growth to be lessened as it has been by those who are not prepared for the experience of guiding children in their growth.

In addition to the material focusing on the adverse effects of individual environments unhealthy for the growth of children, Dr. Montagu guides us to look at the impact of the larger cultural milieu on children not fortu-

* S. Chess, A. Thomas, and H. Birch, *Your Child Is a Person* (New York: The Viking Press, 1965); and L. B. Murphy, *The Widening World of Childhood* (New York: Basic Books, 1962).

nate enough to be born into one of the privileged sectors of our society. He points out the limiting effects on human growth and development of the fallacy that some portions of the human race are better endowed than others. The fact is that although there are physical differences between the various ethnic groups within the human race, there is no evidence that they are paralleled by behavioral differences having a genetic basis. And if there are such differences, there is no reason to believe that they are quantitative in nature—that is, there is no basis for the belief that some peoples are "better" than others. And the effects of such a belief can only be detrimental to the full growth of every individual member of the human race.

It is, of course, easier to attribute our fates to influences not within our control than to accept the fact that responsibility for the state of the human race lies with those in a position to effect change or perpetuate inequities. Those who would justify their judgments about peoples of non-white ethnic groups by attributing their condition to a genetic inferiority are ignoring the real issues and their own responsibilities. We do not know what differences actually exist between the ethnic groups of humankind, if any; what is obvious, however, is that the opportunities provided for the fulfillment of each human being's unique individual development are substantially reduced for those of minority cultures and especially for the children of poverty. There can be no justifiable defense for perpetuating the cycle of poverty. We will all be less as human beings as long as we permit those among us to live in circumstances that prevent their full development as human beings.

We hope the material that follows about the effects of the cultural environment on the growth and development of children will stimulate your thinking about the meaning and relevance of this information to you personally. At the close of the book, in our afterword, we will attempt to focus on insights gained and questions raised by the materials in the volume, and we will ask you, then, to further examine its meaning for you as a human being.

Joseph L. Braga

Laurie D. Braga

General Editors

INTRODUCTION

Culture and Human Development is a book about the effects of human environments upon the growth and development of children—children who grow into adults. It is, therefore, a book about the effects of the man-made environment upon the making of human beings.

For human beings, the principal means of adaptation to the environment is culture, the human-made part of the environment. Most writings in anthropology are designed to show how culture, in all its manifold ways and multifaceted varieties, conditions the behavior of the individual in each society. This constitutes one of the most enlightening contributions of anthropology to humanity.

We have come to understand that cultures differ from one another as a consequence of the differences in the history of experience which they have undergone in more or less isolation from each other. It is the consensus of opinion of students of the matter that the essential likenesses for behavioral achievement among the different ethnic groups or so-called "races" of humankind, are based on fundamental genetic likeness; the behavioral differences we observe among different ethnic groups are principally due to effects of different cultural influences.

This is not to assert anything so foolish as that the human infant is born a *tabula rasa* upon which experience inscribes its directions; nor is any support lent to the spurious "either/or" dissociation between "heredity" and "environment." These terms are, in fact, habitually misused and misunderstood. "Heredity" is not something we inherit; rather, it is the expression of the interaction between our inherited endowment, the genes or genotype, and the environments in which those genes express themselves. Genes do not determine anything. What genes do is, in interaction with the environment, to *influence* the expression of traits.

1

The environment is whatever the organism experiences. It plays an extremely important role in the development of the human species because human beings have to learn everything they come to know and do as human beings. Every human being differs from every other in his genetic constitution. Similar environments may thus come to have different effects on different individuals in accordance with their individual reactive capacities or genetic potentialities. Growth (increase in dimension) and development (increase in complexity) may occur differently in the same environment in different individuals largely because of differences in genetic potentialities. The human child is especially sensitive to environmental influences of a cultural nature, and so, indeed, is the adult.

Culture has undoubtedly been the most important influence in physical as well as mental and social development of human beings; it has also been a most important influence in the growth and development of the individual[1]—and so it continues to be. The contributions presented in this volume constitute eloquent testimony to this latter fact, and it is this area alone with which we are principally concerned in the present volume.

The first contribution of this volume is by Professors Theodosius Dobzhansky, a geneticist, and Ashley Montagu, an anthropologist. They discuss the reasons for thinking it is probable that the mental capacities of humankind are basically similar throughout the species. It is to be understood that capacities refer to potentialities, not to be confused with abilities, which represent *trained* capacities.

There is a strong tendency among some thinkers and writers to believe that a human being is born a *tabula rasa;* this belief leads them to assert that innate influences either do not exist or that they play so minimal a role in the development of the individual they need hardly be considered as factors in the growth and development of his behavior. Whatever conditioning he is exposed to, these thinkers reason, determines what the individual will become. This is an extreme environmentalist viewpoint, and it is unsound. Some writers have found evidence to support this belief in feral children and especially, for some reason, in children supposedly raised by wolves.

---

[1] Ashley Montagu, ed., *Culture and the Evolution of Man* (New York: Oxford University Press, 1962); Ashley Montagu, ed., *Culture: Man's Adaptive Dimension* (New York: Oxford University Press, 1968).

According to such writers' expectations, a child raised by a wolf should behave like a wolf. Such alleged cases have several times been reported, and one that has been most widely quoted in the literature is examined in the second contribution and shown to be quite unacceptable by any scientific standard.

The truth is that we do not require wolf-children to prove to us that cultural conditioning is a most important influence in the development of human behavior. We have to understand that there exist very real biological substrates for behavioral development, but only as potentialities. These potentialities must be experientially trained if they are to function as organized directed acts. It should always be remembered that the existence of biological substrates for human behavior does not mean that human behavior does not have to be learned. It does. Everything a human being comes to do as a human being must be learned. Learning refers to the increase in the strength of any act through repetition, in response to a task situation directly induced by experience.

Speech provides a good illustration of the principle involved. Clearly there exist biological potentialities for speech, without which speech would not be possible, but in order to speak one must learn to speak according to a model provided by the human environment. Apes are wanting in the biological potentialities for speech and therefore cannot be taught to speak. Human beings possess the biological potentialities which make the development of speech possible, but they must experience the stimulation of the human verbal community in order to express that potentiality as a learned ability.

It is important to understand that when one says that everything human beings do must be learned, this does not mean that there are no biological substrates for a given behavior. What it does mean is that, while those biological substrates may influence the development of that behavior, they do not determine it. Development can be defined as an increase in complexity or a sequence of continuous change in the organism over a considerable period of time. The sensitivity and precariousness of the developmental period in human beings is frequently not understood, with consequent great damage to the developing human being.

To illustrate this point, the contribution entitled "The Origin and Significance of Neonatal and Infant Immaturity in Man" draws attention to a new conception of the meaning of gestation and the immature development of the newborn in the human species. Here it is shown that gestation is only half completed when the human infant is born; its immaturity is such that it requires much more careful attention than has hitherto been bestowed upon it, especially in so-called civilized societies. The concepts of gestation within (uterogestation) and gestation outside (exterogestation) the womb, are very important for us to understand, for they represent highly critical periods in the development of the human being; this is especially true of the exterogestative period.

When reference is made to the cultural environment, it is taken for granted that we all understand the same thing by what those words are designed to embrace. But this is seldom the case. When we speak of providing equal opportunities for everyone we tend to think of those opportunities as falling into the categories of equal income for parents, improved standards of living, equal political and social rights, and equal standards of schooling. In the contribution entitled "Just What Is 'Equal Opportunity'?" it is shown that much more is involved; it is explained that the naive application of unexamined concepts may lamentably fail to do justice to the requirements of both the privileged and the underprivileged, but of course, especially the latter; that indeed, the whole concept of "equal opportunity" requires reexamination and redefinition.

In the next contribution, entitled "Sociogenic Brain Damage," the author draws attention to the fact that just as the nervous system of the developing child may be damaged as a consequence of physical malnutrition, so too it may be damaged as a result of cultural or social malnutrition. The experimental evidence on animals is conclusive: impoverished environments produce impoverished brains. There can be little doubt that similar effects are produced upon the developing brain of the child by impoverished human environments.

Such impoverished environments may occur in families in which income, socioeconomic status of the parents, and physical nutrition are adequate, but in which the emotional environment is inadequate. This is dramatically described in the contribution by Drs. Rose W. Coleman and Sally Provence, entitled "Environmental Retardation (Hospitalism) in Infants Living in Families." Here are presented case studies of the children of two unrelated, college-educated mothers. Both children suffered severe physical and mental retardation for no reason other than insufficient maternal care. One cannot help wondering how many such failed children who have gone through life physically and mentally retarded could have been rescued with some tender loving care.

Sociogenic brain damage has been almost completely overlooked as a factor in mental and physical development, but especially in mental development. It has particularly been ignored as a factor in the evaluation of school achievement, and absence of attention to its influence is most apparent in that folly of follies, the misinterpretation of IQ tests as representing a significant statement of the genetic contribution to intelligence.

For many years—from the emergence of the IQ test as an instrument supposedly designed to measure an individual's intellectual capacity, until fairly recently—it was believed that the IQ was a stable measure. For example, a person whose IQ was tested at age eight should, according to this thinking, have approximately the same IQ at age fourteen; people's IQ scores (and presumably their intelligence) were thought to remain the same throughout the years. In fact, for persons whose experiences in life do not change appreciably, there is a great deal of consistency between IQ scores obtained at different times. But, it has been shown conclusively in recent years that changes in the environment can have significant influence on performance on IQ tests. One of the major reasons for this is that IQ tests do not, in fact, measure a person's inherent capacity for learning; rather, they measure how well a person has already learned those things thought to represent intelligence in a particular culture and, perhaps, how well he will learn such things in the future (unless his environment and experiences are significantly changed).

The effects of favorable changes in cultural environment upon performance on IQ tests is strikingly demonstrated in Dr. Thomas R. Garth's brief report on foster Indian children reared in white homes, and by Dr. John H. Rohrer's report on Osage Indians who had achieved socioeconomic advantages equaling those of whites. In both cases (the Navaho Indian children raised in white homes and the Osage children enjoying equal socioeconomic and schooling opportunities with white children), the children did quite as well on the IQ tests as the white children. If anything were necessary to prove the general rule that the quality of cultural experience plays a highly significant role in influencing performance on IQ tests, it would be these two classic reports which, strangely enough, seldom figure in discussions of the subject.[2]

What should be abundantly clear at this late date is that whatever the average IQ performance of a population may be, it is not the performance of populations that should concern us; rather, we should be concerned with the performance of the individual, of every individual within the population.

Further, it is not so much performance with which we should be concerned, but the creation of a society in which every individual is provided with the optimum opportunities for the healthy development of his potentialities, whatever they may be. We mean, by healthy development, development of the ability to love, to work, and to play.

A great deal of attention has been paid in the past to the effects of culture upon the development of functional traits, especially learning ability and intelligence. It has long been known that unfavorable socioeconomic conditions are significantly capable of affecting the physical growth, development, health, and longevity of the individual. But there has been nothing like an equal recognition of the fact that while socioeconomic conditions may superficially appear to be more than adequately favorable for optimum development, there are certain inapparent conditions present which may seriously affect *both* the physical and mental development of the

2 For further discussions of the subject see C. L. Brace, G. R. Gamble, and J. T. Bond, eds., *Race and Intelligence* (Washington, D.C.: American Anthropological Association, 1971); K. Richardson, D. Spears, and M. Richards, eds., *Race, Culture and Intelligence* (Baltimore: Penguin Books, 1972); R. Cancro, ed., *Intelligence: Genetic and Environmental Influences* (New York: Grune & Stratton, 1971); J. McV. Hunt, *Intelligence and Experience* (New York: Ronald Press, 1961); J. McV. Hunt, *The Challenge of Incompetence and Poverty* (Urbana, Ill.: University of Illinois Press, 1969); M. Deutsch, I. Katz, and A. R. Jensen, eds., *Social Class, Race, and Psychological Development* (New York: Holt, Rinehart & Winston, 1968); Ashley Montagu, *Man's Most Dangerous Myth: The Fallacy of Race*, 5th ed. (New York: Oxford University Press, 1974); Ashley Montagu, ed., *Statement on Race* (New York: Oxford University Press, 1972); W. Bodmer and L. L. Cavalli-Sforza, "Intelligence and Race," *Scientific American*, October 1970, pp. 19–29; Ashley Montagu, ed., *Race and IQ* (New York: Oxford University Press, 1975).

individual. I refer here to what, for want of a better name, are called emotional factors.

Among the first to draw attention to the effects of emotional environment upon the growth and development of children was Dr. E. M. Widdowson of the Department of Experimental Medicine at Cambridge University. In what presented itself as a rare unpremeditated experimental opportunity, Dr. Widdowson was able to show, in an unambiguous and quite striking manner, the relation between emotional factors and physical growth and development. This contribution, "Mental Contentment and Physical Growth," is far too little known, and it is hoped that, among other things, its reprinting here will restore it to something of the influence it deserves.

Powell, Brasel, and Blizzard's report, "Emotional Deprivation and Growth Retardation Simulating Idiopathic Hypopituitarism," presents clinical case records that demonstrate the manner in which the endocrine glands responsible for the physical growth and development of children may be affected by emotional factors, resulting in dwarfism. This may be mistaken for an intrinsic failure of secretion of the growth hormones of the pituitary gland, but spontaneous growth resulting simply from a change in environment showed clearly that the problem was emotionally induced and not biologically based. This constitutes a rather dramatic and impressive demonstration of the substantive role played by cultural or emotional factors in the physical *as well as* the behavioral development of the human being. There is now also good evidence that emotional factors mediated through the pregnant mother to the developing embryo are in certain cases capable of producing significant physical changes as well as emotional ones in the fetus, changes which will be evident at birth and after.[3]

A most illuminating account of the subtle manner in which cultural environmental effects may affect the physical and mental growth and development of children is presented by Drs. John B. Reinhart and Allan L. Drash in their contribution "Psychosocial Dwarfism: Environmentally Induced Recovery." Here, the victim is

[3] Ashley Montagu, *Prenatal Influences* (Springfield, Illinois: Charles C Thomas, 1961); Ashley Montagu, *Life Before Birth* (New York: New American Library, 1964).

a girl, a fraternal twin, who from her second to her seventh year was severely retarded in both physical and mental growth. Both her parents abandoned all hope for her and accepted her condition as permanent. She was the only child in the family to be so affected, and it was taken for granted that there was some constitutional defect responsible for her physical and mental retardation. She was sent to a school for handicapped children in which she received special attention. Here, this retarded child began to blossom, so that by the time she was thirteen she had caught up with her normal fraternal twin. The reader is urged to pay particular attention to this report; it discusses some of the kinds of parent-child interactions which often go undetected but which may lead to severely handicapping changes in the child and, it should be added, also in the parents.

In "Sex, Status, Gender, and Cultural Conditioning," the author shows how substantively cultural conditioning influences those "sexual" traits which only too often have been thought to be biologically determined. We tend to confuse biological sex, that is, male or female physical or organic traits with assigned statuses and roles, and most of all with gender, that is, masculinity and femininity, and fail to realize how very little biological sex has to do with what we conceive as gender roles and statuses.

Finally, in "Cultural Deprivation: A Clinical Dimension of Education," Dr. Seymour L. Lustman draws especial attention to the cultural deprivation that the child suffers in the school at the hands of many teachers. One may recall Sir Thomas Elyot's remark in that luminous book on education *The Gouverneur* (1531), "Lorde god, how many good and clene wittes of children be now a dayes perished by ignorant school maisters." Alas. Dr. Lustman, with the added dimensions of his psychological and psychiatric training background continues in the tradition of Elyot in the many wise things he has to say about the child, education, and teachers. His early death at the age of fifty-one is an irreparable loss. It is fitting that this final contribution should serve as a pendant to the present volume.

1
In "Natural Selection and the Mental Capacities of Mankind," Professors Theodosius Dobzhansky, a geneticist, and Ashley Montagu, an anthropologist, pool their knowledge in order to throw some light on the probable selection pressures that were operative in the genetically based behavioral evolution of human beings. Since man lived as a gatherer-hunter for some five or more million years, a period which covers almost the whole of his evolutionary history, it is suggested that the selective pressures for behavioral response to the challenges of the environment were everywhere much alike. Since those pressures were probably so much alike, it would follow that the selection for behavioral traits must also have been very much alike. Therefore it would hardly be expected that any significant differences would have developed in the mental capacities of the different populations of humankind. The differences in such capacities that exist between populations are measured in terms of learned abilities, for an ability is a trained capacity. And such differences in abilities are much more readily explicable as due to differences in the history of experiences undergone by each population than as due to genetic differences.

This selection was chosen to begin the volume because it introduces the influence, historically, of culture on the development of human beings. It highlights the fact that the most outstanding feature of human beings is their plasticity, their educability. What this means is that, within the range of what is possible according to their biological capacities, human beings will adapt to whatever they are exposed to experientially. This is both encouraging and disturbing. It is encouraging because it gives us hope that if we can change the human environment in desirable ways, we will also positively affect the development of individual human beings and, therefore, also the species as a whole. But it is disturbing when one considers the inhuman and inhumane environments to which human beings can be forced to adapt.

"Natural Selection and the Mental Capacities of Mankind" by Theodosius Dobzhansky and Ashley Montagu. From *Science,* vol. 105, June 6, 1947, pp. 587–90. Reprinted by permission of the authors and *Science.*

9

NATURAL SELECTION AND THE MENTAL CAPACITIES OF MANKIND

Theodosius Dobzhansky
and Ashley Montagu

The fundamental mechanisms of the transmission of heredity from parents to offspring are surprisingly uniform in most diverse organisms. Their uniformity is perhaps the most remarkable fact disclosed by genetics. The laws discovered by Mendel apply to human genes just as much as to those of the maize plant, and the processes of cellular division and germ cell maturation in man are not very different from those in a grasshopper. The similarity of the mechanisms of heredity on the individual level is reflected on the population level in a similarity of the basic causative factors of organic evolution throughout the living world. Mutation, selection, and genetic drift are important in the evolution of man as well as in amoebae and in bacteria. Wherever sexuality and cross-fertilization are established as exclusive or predominant methods of reproduction, the field of hereditary variability increases enormously as compared with asexual or self-fertilizing organisms. Isolating mechanisms which prevent interbreeding and fusion of species of mammals are operative also among insects.

Nevertheless, the universality of basic genetic mechanisms and of evolutionary agents permits a variety of evolutionary patterns to exist not only in different lines of descent but even at different times in the same line of descent. It is evident that the evolutionary pattern in the dog species under domestication is not the same as in the wild ancestors of the domestic dogs or in the now living wild relatives. Widespread occurrence of reduplication of chromosome complements (polyploidy) in the evolution of plants introduces complexities which are not found in the animal kingdom, where polyploidy is infrequent. Evolutionary situations among parasites and among cave inhabitants are clearly different from those in free-living forms. Detection and analysis of differences in the evolutionary patterns in different organisms is one of the important tasks of modern evolutionists.

It can scarcely be doubted that man's biological heredity is transmitted by mechanisms similar to those encountered in other animals and in plants. Likewise, there is no reason to believe that the evolutionary development of man has involved causative factors other than those operative in the evolution of other organisms. The evolutionary changes that occurred before the prehuman could become human, as well as those which supervened since the attainment of the human estate, can be described causally only in terms of mutation, selection, genetic drift, and hybridization—familiar processes throughout the living world. This reasoning, indisputable in the purely biological context, becomes a fallacy, however, when used, as it often has been, to justify narrow biologism in dealing with human material.

The specific human features of the evolutionary pattern of man cannot be ignored. Man is a unique product of evolution in that he, far more than any other creature, has escaped from the bondage of the physical and the biological into the multiform social environment. This remarkable development introduces a third dimension in addition to those of the external and internal environments— a dimension which many biologists, in considering the evolution of man, tend to neglect. The most important setting of human evolution is the human social environment. As stated above, this can influence evolutionary changes only through the media of mutation, selection, genetic drift, and hybridization. Nevertheless, there can be no genuine clarity in our understanding of man's biological nature until the role of the social factor in the development of the human species is understood. A biologist approaching the problems of human evolution must never lose sight of the truth stated more than 2,000 years ago by Aristotle: "Man is by nature a political animal."

In the words of R. A. Fisher, "For rational systems of evolution, that is, for theories which make at least the most familiar facts intelligible to the reason, we must turn to those that make progressive adaptation the driving force of the process." It is evident that man by means of his reasoning abilities, by becoming a "political animal," has achieved a mastery of the world's varying environments quite unprecedented in the history of organic evolution. The system of genes which has permitted the development of the specifically human mental capacities has thus become the foundation and the paramount influence in all subsequent evolution of the human stock. An animal becomes adapted to its environment by evolving certain genetically determined physical and behavioral traits; the adaptation of man consists chiefly in developing his inventiveness, a quality to which his physical heredity predisposes him and which his social heredity provides him with the means of realizing. To the degree to which this is so, man is unique. As far as his physical responses to the world are concerned, he is almost wholly emancipated from dependence upon inherited biological dispositions, uniquely improving upon the latter by the process of learning that which his social heredity (culture) makes available to him. Man possesses much more efficient means of achieving immediate or long-term adaptation than any other biological species: namely, through learned responses or novel inventions and improvisations.

In general, two types of biological adaptation in evolution can be distinguished. One is genetic specialization and genetically controlled fixity of traits. The second consists in the ability to respond to a given range of environmental situations by evolving traits favorable in these particular situations; this presupposes genetically controlled plasticity of traits. It is known, for example, that the composition of the blood which is most favorable for life at high altitudes is somewhat different from that which suffices at sea level. A species which ranges from sea level to high altitudes on a mountain range may become differentiated into several altitudinal races, each having a fixed blood composition favored by natural selection at the particular altitude at which it lives; or a genotype may be selected which permits an individual to respond to changes in the atmospheric pressure by definite alterations in the composition of the blood. It is well known that heredity determines in its possessor not the presence or absence of certain traits but, rather, the responses of the organisms to its environments. The responses may be more or less rigidly fixed, so that approximately the same traits develop in all environments in which life is possible. On the other hand, the responses may differ in different environments. Fixity or plasticity of a trait is, therefore, genetically controlled.

Whether the evolutionary adaptation in a given phyletic line will occur chiefly by way of genetic fixity or by way of genetically controlled plasticity of traits will depend on circumstances. In the first place, evolutionary changes are compounded of mutational steps, and consequently the kind of change that takes place is always determined by the composition of the store of mutational variability which happens to be available in the species populations. Secondly, fixity or plasticity of traits is controlled by natural selection. Having a trait fixed by heredity and hence appearing in the development of an individual regardless of environmental variations is, in general, of benefit to organisms whose milieu remains uniform and static except for rare and freakish deviations. Conversely, organisms which inhabit changeable environments are benefited by having their traits plastic and modified by each recurrent configuration of environmental agents in a way most favorable for the survival of the carrier of the trait in question.

Comparative anatomy and embryology show that a fairly general trend in organic evolution seems to be from environmental dependence toward fixation of the basic features of the bodily structure and function. The appearance of these structural features in the embryonic development of higher organisms is, in general, more nearly autonomous and independent of the environment than in lower forms. The development becomes "buffered" against environmental and genetic shocks. If, however, the mode of life of a species happens to be such that it is, of necessity, exposed to a wide range of environments, it becomes desirable to vary some structures and functions in accordance with the circumstances that confront an individual or a strain at a given time and place. Genetic structures which permit adaptive plasticity of traits become, then, obviously advantageous for survival and so are fostered by natural selection.

The social environments that human beings have created everywhere are notable not only for their extreme complexity but also for the rapid changes to which immediate adjustment is demanded. Adjustment occurs chiefly in the psychical realm and has little or nothing to do with physical traits. In view of the fact that from the very beginning of human evolution the changes in the human environment have been not only rapid but diverse and manifold, genetic fixation of behavioral traits in man would have been decidedly unfavorable for survival of individuals as well as of the species as a whole. Success of the individual in most human societies has depended and continues to depend upon his ability rapidly to evolve behavior patterns which fit him to the kaleidoscope of the conditions he encounters. He is best off if he submits to some, compromises with some, rebels against others, and escapes from still other situations. Individuals who display a relatively greater fixity of response than their fellows suffer under most forms of human society and tend to fall by the way. Suppleness, plasticity, and, most important of all, ability to profit by experience and education are required. No other species is comparable to man in its capacity to acquire new behavior patterns and discard old ones in consequence of training. Considered socially as well as biologically, man's outstanding capacity is his educability. The survival value of this capacity is manifest, and therefore the possibility of its development through natural selection is evident.

It should be made clear at this point that the replacement of fixity of behavior by genetically controlled plasticity is not a necessary consequence of all forms of social organization. The quaint attempts to glorify insect societies as examples deserving emulation on the part of man ignore the fact that the behavior of an individual among social insects is remarkable precisely because of the rigidity of its genetic fixation. The perfection of the organized societies of ants, termites, bees, and other insects is indeed wonderful, and the activities of their members may strike an observer very forcibly by their objective purposefulness. This purposefulness is retained, however, only in environments in which the species normally lives. The ability of an ant to adjust its activities to situations not encountered in the normal habitats of its species is very limited. On the other hand, social organizations on the human level are built on the principle that an individual is able to alter his behavior to fit any situation, whether previously experienced or new.

This difference between human and insect societies is, of course, not surprising. Adaptive plasticity of behavior can develop not only on the basis of a vastly more complex nervous system than is sufficient for adaptive fixity. The genetic differences between human and insect societies furnish a striking illustration of the two types of evolutionary adaptations—those achieved through genetically controlled plasticity of behavioral traits and those attained through genetic specialization and fixation of behavior.

The genetically controlled plasticity of mental traits is, biologically speaking, the most typical and uniquely human characteristic. It is very probable that the survival value of this characteristic in human evolution has been considerable for a long time, as measured in terms of human historical scales. Just when this characteristic first appeared is, of course, conjectural. Here it is of interest to note that the most marked phylogenetic trend in the evolution of man has been the special development of the brain, and that the characteristic human plasticity of mental traits seems to be associated with the exceptionally large brain size. The brain of, for example, the Lower or Middle Pleistocene fossil forms of man was, grossly at least, scarcely distinguishable from that of modern man. The average Neanderthaloid brain was somewhat larger than that of modern man, though slightly different in shape. More important than the evidence derived from brain size is the testimony of cultural development. The Middle Acheulean handiwork of Swanscombe man of several hundred thousand years ago and the beautiful Mousterian cultural artifacts associated with Neanderthal man indicate the existence of minds of a high order of development.

The cultural evidence thus suggests that the essentially human organization of the mental capacities emerged quite early in the evolution of man. However that may be, the possession of the gene system, which conditions educability rather than behavioral fixity, is a common property of all living mankind. In other words, educability is truly a species character of man, *Homo sapiens.* This does not mean, of course, that the evolutionary process has run its course and that natural selection has introduced no changes in the genetic structure of the human species since the attainment of the human status. Nor do we wish to imply that no genetic variations in mental equipment exist at our time level. On the contrary, it seems likely that with the attainment of human status that part of man's genetic system which is related to mental potentialities did not cease to be labile and subject to change.

This brings us face to face with the old problem of the likelihood that significant genetic differences in the mental capacities of the various ethnic groups of mankind exist. The physical and, even more, the social environments of men who live in different countries are quite diversified. Therefore, it has often been argued, natural selection would be expected to differentiate the human species into local races differing in psychic traits. Populations of different countries may differ in skin color, head shape, and other somatic characters. Why, then, should they be alike in mental traits?

It will be through investigation rather than speculation that the problem of the possible existence of average differences in the mental make-up of human populations of different geographical origins will eventually be settled. Arguments based on analogies are precarious, especially where evolutionary patterns are concerned. If human races differ in structural traits, it does not necessarily follow that they must also differ in mental ones. Race differences arise chiefly because of the differential action of natural selection on geographically separated populations. In the case of man, however, the structural and mental traits are quite likely to be influenced by selection in different ways.

The very complex problem of the origin of racial differentiations in structural traits does not directly concern us here. Suffice it to say that racial differences in traits such as the blood groups may conceivably have been brought about by genetic drift in populations of limited effective size. Other racial traits are genetically too complex and too consistently present in populations of some large territories and absent in other territories to be accounted for by genetic drift alone. Differences in skin color, hair form, nose shape, etc. are almost certainly products of natural selection. The lack of reliable knowledge of the adaptive significance of these traits is perhaps the greatest gap in our understanding of the evolutionary biology of man. Nevertheless, it is at least a plausible working hypothesis that these and similar traits have, or at any rate had in the past, differential survival values in the environments of different parts of the world.

By contrast, the survival value of a higher development of mental capacities in man is obvious. Furthermore, natural selection seemingly favors such a development everywhere. In the ordinary course of events in almost all societies those persons are likely to be favored who show wisdom, maturity of judgment, and ability to get along with people—qualities which may assume different forms in different cultures. Those are the qualities of the plastic personality, not a single trait but a general condition, and this is the condition which appears to have been at a premium in practically all human societies.

In human societies conditions have been neither rigid nor stable enough to permit the selective breeding of genetic types adapted to different statuses or forms of social organization. Such rigidity and stability do not obtain in any society. On the other hand, the outstanding fact about human societies is that they do change and do so more or less rapidly. The rate of change was possibly comparatively slow in earlier societies, as the rate of change in present-day nonliterate societies may be, when compared to the rate characterizing occidental societies. In any event, rapid changes in behavior are demanded of the person at all levels of social organization even when the society is at its most stable. Life at any level of social development in human societies is a pretty complex business, and it is met and handled most efficiently by those who exhibit the greatest capacity for adaptability, plasticity.

It is this very plasticity of his mental traits which confers upon man the unique position which he occupies in the animal kingdom. Its acquisition freed him from the constraint of a limited range of biologically predetermined responses. He became capable of acting in a more or less regulative manner upon his physical environment instead of being largely regulated by it. The process of natural selection in all climes and at all times have favored genotypes which permit greater and greater educability and plasticity of mental traits under the influence of the uniquely social environments to which man has been continuously exposed.

The effect of natural selection in man has probably been to render genotypic differences in personality traits, as between individuals and particularly as between races, relatively unimportant compared to their phenotypic plasticity. Instead of having his responses genetically fixed as in other animal species, man is a species that invents its own responses, and it is out of this unique ability to invent, to improvise, his responses that his cultures are born.

2 In the foregoing selection, it was argued that the genetic differences underlying behavioral differences between human populations are minimal, and that man's principal mode of adaptation is through responses learned from the man-made part of the environment. Thus, human beings are capable of developing diverse behaviors within the range of what is humanly possible, biologically and socially. But there are some who have carried this awareness of the impact of the environment upon human development to unsupportable extremes. Ignoring the biological and social conditions of human development, they have gone so far as to assert that a human being will become *anything* that he or she experiences, even to the extent of becoming animal-like when raised by animals. This is, in fact, quite untrue. There is no evidence to support such claims. And, as will be seen in the selection following this one, human infants require much more care and nurturance than it would be possible for any nonhuman animal to provide.

Stories of children who have been raised by animals are well-nigh universal. They have formed part of the folklore of many peoples. It will be recalled that the legendary founders of Rome, Romulus and Remus, were said to have been reared by a she-wolf. Rudyard Kipling based his Mowgli stories on tales of children in India who had allegedly been raised by animals. In many parts of the world today women of non-literate societies will suckle small animals at the breast, often while giving the other breast to their own child. It does not seem so strange, therefore, that the practice should sometimes be thought to be reversible, and that animals should be believed capable of suckling human infants. Hence, every so often reports appear in the press and in the literature of a new "wolf-child," or "baboon-boy," who has allegedly been raised by one of these animals. Upon investigation these cases invariably prove to be either false or unprovable. Nevertheless, a fair number of scientists, on very slender grounds indeed, have been persuaded that in one or two cases the evidence was compelling enough for them to vouch for the truth of wolf-raised children.

The scientific attitude of mind is characterized by a desire

"Wolf Children" by Ashley Montagu. Reprinted from the *American Anthropologist*, n.s. vol. 45 (1943), pp. 468–72.

neither to believe nor to disbelieve, but by the desire to discover what is. The method of discovering what is, is essentially verification. If we can check the facts there is the possibility of arriving at a sound judgment, but if we cannot check them we had better suspend judgment till either we ourselves or someone else has had the opportunity of checking them.

The facts concerning feral children or animal-raised children have now been fully checked, and the conclusion is unequivocally clear that in not a single case have the claims for the existence of such children been substantiated. Children who have been more or less isolated from association with other human beings have been described and verified, and their study has been quite illuminating (Note 1). But such children are quite a different kettle of fish from allegedly animal-raised children. What is claimed for children allegedly raised by animals is that they have taken on the behavioral traits of their putative animal socializers—very much as, according to one extreme environmentalist theory, one would expect. Writers who believe that man has no nature, but only a history, claim that it is the history of his social experience that will determine what he becomes behaviorally; hence, when children are brought up by wolves, they behave like wolves, and they even develop some physical traits, it is alleged, that are lupine.

I have discussed these claims in the contribution which follows. This was originally published as a review of a book on a supposedly newly discovered pair of "wolf-children" which dealt also with several classical reports on feral man (Note 2). Shortly afterwards Bergen Evans published a devastating critique, "Wolf! Wolf!", of the same book, in his *The Natural History of Nonsense* (Note 3). In spite of these two thoroughgoing demolitions, the story of Amala and Kamala, the wolf-children of "Midnapore," has found wide acceptance among uncritical sociologists and others. As late as the end of 1973 a textbook on sociology reproduced the story as if no one had ever questioned it. My review is reprinted here both as a cautionary homily and as a statement of the fact that there is not the slightest evidence for the belief that any animal has ever raised a human infant or ever could do so. The probabilities are utterly against such a possibility—not because of any fancied unwillingness on the part of any animal to do so, but because of the constitutional weakness and immaturity of the human infant, its great delicacy, its comparative inability to cling, and the especially delicate care it requires for survival. No animal would be able to provide this. To become human requires more than human biology; it requires also human nurturance and socialization. This is a subject which is, in part, dealt with in the contribution which follows.

The importance of this selection to the volume is to remind the reader of the interrelation between human nature and human nurture. The human infant is biologically oriented to develop only within the context of a human environment and all that accompanies it. The plasticity of human beings is such that human behavioral traits can be realized only within the limits of the variety, requirements, and possibilities of a human culture. That plasticity does not extend to the limit of a human infant becoming anything other than a human being. Raised outside the context of human culture, a human infant could not become part of another animal culture. It would simply perish.

NOTE 1: For an account of these see Ashley Montagu, *The Direction of Human Development* (New York: Hawthorn Books, 1970). NOTE 2: J. A. L. Singh and Robert M. Zingg, *Wolf-Children and Feral Man* (New York: Harper & Bros., 1942). NOTE 3: (New York: A. A. Knopf, 1946), pp. 86–99.

"WOLF CHILDREN"

Ashley Montagu

In 1941 Professor Arnold Gesell of the Clinic of Child Development, Yale University, published a book entitled *Wolf Child and Human Child, Being a Narrative Interpretation of the Life History of Kamala, the Wolf Girl.* A few months later, in 1942, Professor Robert M. Zingg, then of the University of Denver, published a book entitled *Wolf-Children and Feral Man,* his coauthor being the Reverend J. A. L. Singh.

These two books at once brought to the attention of the public the existence of the first "authenticated wolf children," children who had been, so it was claimed, raised by wolves. During the thirty years since the advent of the wolf children was announced to the world, they have steadily crept into the literature on all fours as genuine examples of human beings raised by animals.

The story of Kamala and Amala, the wolf children of "Godamuri" or of Midnapore, constitutes an interesting study in scientific credulity. Very briefly, two children were claimed to have been repeatedly seen by natives and other villagers emerging together with several wolves from the ant-hill den of the said wolves. The Reverend J. A. L. Singh states that, while traveling in the company of two Anglo-Indians who were witnesses to the event, he captured or liberated the two children from the wolves' den at Godamuri on October 17, 1920. At the time of their rescue, or liberation, the younger child was guessed to be about eighteen months old. She was given the name Amala. The older child was estimated to be about eight years of age, and was named Kamala. It is assumed that both children were about six months of age when taken by the wolves, and that they were stolen from different families. Amala died on September 21, 1921, while Kamala died November 14, 1929. Thus Amala was observed for almost a year and Kamala for nine years.

When first observed, Kamala and Amala were unable to stand in the erect position but habitually progressed on all fours. They ate raw meat and entrails in what is alleged to have been wolf fashion, were without sphincter control, howled like wolves, preferred the society of dogs to that of human beings, and exhibited other feral traits. They were entirely without speech and all those other attributes which we have come to regard as specifically human. . . .

In *Wolf-Children and Feral Man* Dr. Robert Zingg makes available an account of the history of these children written by the Reverend J. A. L. Singh based upon the records which the latter kept while the children were under his own and his wife's observation in their orphanage at Midnapore. In the second part of the work Dr. Zingg discusses the subject of feral man in general and records a number of cases of extreme isolation of children in particular, the latter for their own interest and also in order to serve as checks against the description of the behavior of the "wolf children." There are forewords by Professors R. Ruggles Gates, Arnold Gesell, Francis

N. Maxfield, and Kingsley Davis, each attesting his belief in the genuineness of the discovery and the account of the children as given by the Reverent Singh. A preface by Bishop H. Pakenham-Walsh, together with an affidavit by the District Judge of Midnapore, E. Waight, to both of whom the Reverend Singh was well known, testifies to his good character and reliability and their belief in the truth of his account of the discovery of the "wolf children."

Let me say that having read the volume very critically I find that despite certain difficulties, the Reverend Singh's account of his discovery and observations has an impressive ring of authenticity about it. The writer impresses me as a naïve but honest person who records his observation frankly, while even those which seem to belong to the realm of folklore, rather than to that of sober fact, read quite as convincingly as those which do not seem to be either a little east or a little west of the truth.

But when all this has been said, it must regretfully be added that this account of the "wolf children" cannot be accepted as true. I say "regretfully" for several reasons. Firstly, because I should very much like to believe the greater part of this story since it appears to fit into the general theory of personal social development fairly well, and we should at long last have at least one authentic case of children reared by animals with which to support our theories. Secondly, because I have a private Franciscan belief in the fellowship of man with all nature which I should like to have seen supported by so striking an instance. But as Mr. Pecksniff would have said, "Facts is facts." And the facts in this book, alas, rest on the completely unsupported testimony of one person, the Reverend Singh. Now, however much and however sympathetically we might be inclined to put our trust in his word, no scientist can accept as true any statement of a fellow scientist or the statement of anyone else until it has been independently confirmed by others. Such confirmation is altogether wanting in the present case, and that being so, with all the good will in the world and in spite of all the prefaces and forewords by learned professors, bishops, and magistrates, we cannot accept as true the story of the discovery of the "wolf children" and their presumed rearing by wolves.

The process of verification and confirmation is a cardinal princi-

ple of scientific method, the method of arriving at scientifically sup-
portable results. Whether or not children have been reared by animals can be determined only by observation not necessarily pre-
meditated and carried out under conditions which provide the means
of verification. Hundreds of stories and legends say that they have
been so reared, and the investigation of these stories constitutes a
legitimate and scientific activity. Dr. Zingg has been interested in
examining such stories for some time, with not altogether happy results. It seems to me that in the present volume he is not so much
concerned with an impartial examination of the evidence as with
insisting upon one interpretation of it. I regret to have to say this
because I have every sympathy for the enthusiast, and it is quite
understandable that once having become enamored of a story one
might be carried away by it. But this is just the sort of thing against
which even the best of scientists must continually be on their guard.
Even scientific structures are sometimes erected on emotional foundations. Emotionally I might favor the Singh-Zingg & Co. story; as a
scientist I cannot accept it.

Even if the whole story were better authenticated, here are a few
points which would cause me to make some reservations:

Two Anglo-Indians, a Mr. P. Rose and a Mr. Henry Richards, are
said by the Reverend Singh to have witnessed the rescue of the children from the wolves' den, but unfortunately the former is now un-
traceable and the latter is dead. Why, during all the years the Reverend Singh was studying the children, did he make no attempt to
obtain statements from these and other men who were present at the
alleged rescue? Neither Mr. Rose nor Mr. Richards ever came for-
ward to avow or disavow the Reverend Singh's story.

Kamala is presumed to have been kept in the wolves' den for
about seven and a half years. But wolves do not keep their young
for anything like so long a period under normal conditions. Is it
likely that they would have departed from the universal practice of
wolves in the case of Kamala?

Could a six-month-old child be suckled by a wolf? It is, no doubt,
possible, but it is difficult to imagine why a wolf should want to do
such a troublesome thing.

Even if the statement were fully corroborated that the children were found together with the wolves in their den, that in itself would not constitute evidence that they were brought there by wolves nor that they had been suckled and reared by them.

The Reverend Singh states that Kamala and Amala used to howl regularly almost every night at about ten o'clock, and at one and three o'clock in the morning. The fact is that the idea that wolves howl at regular hours every night is a widespread folk belief not borne out by the observation of wolves' habits. So that what was obviously intended as an irrefutable indication of the children's lupine nature serves, rather, to arouse further doubts as to the accuracy of the narrative.

The statement that the children were not observed to sweat is yet another example of the obvious influence of folkloristic belief upon the Reverend Singh's narrative. The widespread notion that dogs do not sweat except through the tongue is quite untrue; dogs possess numerous sweat glands on every part of the body. But for the purposes of the Reverend Singh's narrative, since dogs and wolves are closely related—and since the wolf children were alleged to have adopted the habits of wolves—it must follow that the wolf children did not sweat.

The eyes of the children are said to have emitted a blue light at night. "Night glare" is a phenomenon not unknown in human beings, but it is a condition of such great rarity that the chances against its ever occurring in two individuals living together are so astronomically high that we are forced to give up all attempt at normal explanation. The necessary extreme myopia or hypermetropia may have been present, but there is very definitely no evidence of any such condition in the Reverend Singh's account. I have been unable to find any record of children who were brought up in darkness exhibiting a like phenomenon. It is difficult to conceive of the special structure necessary, the tapetum (the iridescent layer of the choroid coat of the eye of certain carnivorous animals), developing as a special adaptation to the conditions of life of Kamala and Amala. But what is even more difficult to conceive is the emission of "a peculiar blue glare, like that of a cat or a dog, in the dark" without the presence, as far as one can gather, of any external source of light. This is, in fact, quite impossible, for the light must always be of external origin and is only reflected back by the eye. It was an old Arab belief that the eye itself emitted light! As for the "blue" glare itself, this would appear to be impossible in the case of human beings for the simple reason that the only possible source of such "glaring" is the fundus (the posterior portion or base of the eye), and this normally reflects either a dark red, or an orange-yellow color. The blue eye glare of cats and dogs, and many other animals, is due to the refraction of particles in the tapetum similar to those which in the human iris produce the appearance of the normal blue eye, but which have no connection in the latter case with "night glare." In the offspring of Malayan-Negro crosses, the fundus, through the ophthalmoscope, may appear somewhat bluish, or even gray, depending upon the presence of certain pigment particles, but it is doubtful whether in such cases one could obtain a bluish or grayish glare from the eyes. It is of significance to note that all the supporting cases cited by Dr. Zingg gave either a dark red or, as in the case referred to by Parsons, "a yellow reflex from the pupil." But the latter case refers specifically to the presence of glioma of the retina.

There are other difficulties which could be similarly discussed. But let us come to the point. The Reverend Singh claimed that Amala and Kamala were reared by wolves. What evidence exists in support of his claim? The answer is *none*. The grounds upon which this answer is based have already been briefly stated.

Were Amala and Kamala abandoned by their parents? No one knows. Were these children congenitally defective in any way? It is impossible to say. If they were not congenitally defective, then it would be a reasonable inference to make that their retardation, or rather nondevelopment as human beings, was due to the fact that during the critical period of their development they were practically entirely isolated from the conditioning influences of human contacts. It is during this conditioning period that it is assumed they spent their lives with wolves, living the life of wolves, so that behaviorally they became what they were assumed to have been exposed to—wolves.

On that point we must suspend judgment, but taking the matter from the general standpoint of the development of behavior one thing is certain: Given all the necessary normal potentialities an individual does not become a functioning human being simply by virtue of being born into the species *Homo sapiens;* indeed, he cannot become a functioning human being until he is exposed to the humanizing influences of other human beings. The attributes of humanity are a function of human society, of human socializing factors acting upon potentialities capable of being humanized.

Dr. Zingg writes that "radicals" who believe that "environment completely molds the human mind and mentality . . . overlook the fact that mentality is a bioneurological mechanism, and mind, the environmentally conditioned content organized by that mechanism. Though here we see a well-attested case of human beings reduced to wolf-conditioning, the radical case still needs a case of a wolf raised to human behavior."

Dr. Zingg may be allowed a distinction between "mind" and "mentality," though I do not know what that distinction may be, but he certainly entertains some strange notions on the nature of what "radicals" are supposed to believe. Dr. Zingg disagrees with the straw men of his own making that a wolf or other animal could be "educated into the behavior of a man." But surely, whatever Rousseau or the ingenious Monboddo may have thought, no one today, not even the "radicals," believes anything else than that it is utterly impossible to make a human mind out of the cellular characters of the nervous system of any nonhominid animal. The bioneurological potentialities of such animals do not possess the necessary qualities.

As for Dr. Zingg's statement that mentality may be regarded as the environmentally conditioned content organized by the bioneurological mechanism, I am not sure that he is not right. But is it not perhaps more in accord with the evidence to say that mind represents the environmental organization—or, better, integration—of the bioneurological mechanism? Does behavior represent the bioneurological organization of environmentally conditioned contents or do the environmentally conditioned contents acting upon a relatively undifferentiated variety of nervous tissues serve to differentiate and organize those tissues into a bioneurological system which then functions as mind? The truth, perhaps, lies somewhere between the two views.

I believe that the work of cultural anthropologists, and of experimental biologists and psychologists, would favor the second view.

As Coghill has remarked in the final sentence of that most fundamental of all works on the subject, *Anatomy and the Problem of
Behaviour,* "Man is, indeed, a mechanism, but he is a mechanism
which, within his limitations of life, sensitivity, and growth, is creating and operating himself."

Since the above was written, Doctors W. F. Ogburn and N. K. Bose
have made a thorough on-the-spot investigation of the story of the
wolf children. The findings of these investigators indicate that while
two children named Amala and Kamala lived for a time in the Singh
orphanage, there is no evidence whatever to support the account
given of these children's "history" by Singh and Zingg. Even the vil-
lage, "Godamuri," the alleged site of the wolves' den, does not exist
in Midnapore or anywhere else in India.[1]

1 Ogburn, W. F. and Bose, N. K. "On the Trail of the Wolf Children," *Genetic
Psychology Monographs,* vol. 60, 1959 (pp. 117–193).

3 In the preceding selection, the possibility of human infants being raised by animals was dismissed on the grounds that there is no real evidence to support such claims. The reliability of such accounts was questioned for a very valid reason. Because of the extreme immaturity of the human infant at birth, it requires a human caregiver in order to survive. In the following selection, it is proposed that, in fact, the first nine months after birth constitute a stage in growth that parallels that of the nine months spent in the womb. The evidence is discussed for the hypothesis that the gestation period of the human infant is only half completed at birth, and that it takes about an equal amount of time—that is to say, another 267 days—outside the womb before gestation is fully completed. The human infant must be born when it is because if it were not its head would be unable to pass through the birth canal. It is very immature at birth and still has much growing to do before it can control its own movements, eat solid food, and so on.

For those concerned with human development, the important fact is that the human infant is born in a very much more immature state of development than has hitherto been understood. This period, beginning at birth and lasting about nine months, which I have called *exterogestation,* in contrast to *uterogestation,* the period the conceptus spends in the womb, is a very critical one, during which the infant requires an especial amount and quality of tender loving care (Note 1). The care needed by the infant in the first nine months after birth must reflect an appreciation of the requirements of this period for the child's growth.

The prolongation of the gestation period constitutes yet another example of *neoteny,* the evolutionary process by which development proceeds in a species by the retention of ancestral fetal or juvenile traits into adult stages of development. Examples of physical neoteny in humans are the large head, flatness of face, long neck, large volume of brain, roundheadedness, thinness of skull bones, late eruption of teeth, relative hairlessness of body, playfulness, fun-loving, curiosity, inventiveness, and imaginativeness (Note 2).

"The Origin and Significance of Neonatal and Infant Immaturity in Man" by Ashley Montagu. From the *Journal of the American Medical Association,* vol. 178 (1961), pp. 156–57. Reprinted by permission of the author and the publisher.

The important thing is to die young—as late as possible.

NOTE 1: See Ashley Montagu, *Touching* (New York: Columbia University Press, 1971); and in paperback (New York: Harper & Row, Perennial Books, 1972). NOTE 2: G. de Beer, *Embryos and Ancestors,* 3rd ed. (New York: Oxford University Press, 1958).

THE ORIGIN AND SIGNIFICANCE OF NEONATAL AND INFANT IMMATURITY IN MAN

Ashley Montagu

Why are human beings born in a state so immature that it takes 8 to 10 months before the human infant can even crawl, and another 4 to 6 months before he can walk and talk? That a good many years will elapse before the human child will cease to depend upon others for his very survival constitutes yet another evidence of the fact that man is born and remains more immature for a longer period than any other animal.

The newborn elephant and the fallow deer can run with the herd shortly after they are born. By the age of 6 weeks, the infant seal has been taught by his mother to navigate his watery world for himself. These animals all have long gestation periods, presumably because animals that give birth to small litters, which they are unable to protect as efficiently as predatory animals can, must give birth to young who are in a fairly mature state. A long gestation period serves to allow for such maturation.

The elephant, which has a gestation period of 515 to 670 days, is monotocous, having but one young at a birth. In the polytocous fallow deer, which has 2 or 3 young at a birth, the gestation period is 230 days, and in the seal, which produces only a single pup at a birth, the gestation period varies from 245 to 350 days. Predatory animals, by contrast, are very efficient in protecting their young, and have a short gestation period. Their litters can vary from 3 upwards; the size of the young can be small at birth, and the young can be born in a somewhat immature state. The lion, for example, which generally has a litter of 3 pups, has a gestation period of 105 days. Man has a gestation period of 267 days, which is distinctly in the class of long gestation periods. Since this is so, what can be the reason that man is born in so extremely immature a state? Quite clearly the human infant arrives in the world long before he becomes ready to take it on for himself. How has this come about?

The hypothesis proposed here is that man is born as immaturely as he is because—owing to the great increase in the size of his brain and consequently of his head—if he weren't born when he is, he wouldn't be born at all. As a result of discoveries made during the last 40 years, it now seems probable that during the early evolution of man, several important changes occurred simultaneously. In adaptation to the novel changes presented by the translation from a forest environment to the open plains—associated with the development of a tool-making, hunting economy, and the accompanying high premium placed upon the development of the erect bipedal gait—the brain grew larger while the pelvic outlet grew smaller. At birth the average volume of the brain is 350 cc. Were that volume to increase only slightly, the head could not pass through the birth canal. As it is, in many cases, the size of the baby's head constitutes a hazard to both baby and mother. The rate of growth of the brain is proceeding at such a rate that it cannot continue within the womb and must continue outside the womb. In other words, the survival of the fetus and mother requires the termination of gestation within the womb (uterogestation or interogestation) when the limit of head size compatible with birth has been reached, and long before maturation occurs.

Gestation, then, is not completed by the act of birth but is only translated from gestation within the womb to gestation outside the womb (exterogestation). Professor John Bostock of the University of Queensland, Australia, has suggested that the limit of exterogestation be set at the stage of development of effective locomotion on all fours, a suggestion which has a good deal of merit. According to this hypothesis, man spends the first half of his gestation period within the womb (uterogestation), and the second half of it outside the womb (exterogestation).

It is of interest to note that the average duration of exterogestation—that is, the period from birth to the development of quadrupedal locomotion—lasts exactly the same time, on the average, as the period of uterogestation, namely, 267 days. In connection with this, it is also to be noted that, while the mother nurses her infant, pregnancy will not usually occur for at least 267 days after the birth of the child.

To learn what the child must learn in order to function as an adequate human being, he must have a large brain. It is a striking fact that by the time the human child has attained its third birthday it has also virtually achieved the full adult size of the brain. The brain volume of the human three-year-old is 1,250 cc, while the brain volume of the human adult is 1,400 cc. Significantly, the human brain more than doubles in size during its first year of development, attaining, on the average, a volume of 800 cc. About two-thirds of the total growth of the brain is achieved by the end of the first year, and it will take an additional 2 years to accomplish the same amount of growth, that is, to 1,250 cc. In its first year, the infant's brain does more growing than it will ever do again in any one year.

It is important that most of the brain growth be accomplished during the first year, when the infant has so much to learn and do, for the first year of life requires a great deal of unobtrusive packing for a journey that will last the rest of the traveler's life. To perform this packing successfully, his brain must be much larger than 350 cc, but quite clearly he cannot wait till he has grown a brain of 800 cc before being born. Hence, he must be born with the maximum-sized brain possible, and do the rest of his brain growing after birth. Since the human fetus must be born when its brain has reached the limit of size compatible with its passage through the birth canal, such maturation or further development as other mammals complete before birth the human mammal will have to complete after birth. In other words, the gestation period will have to be extended beyond birth.

If this interpretation of the gestation period is sound, then it would follow that we are not at present meeting the needs of infants in anything approaching an adequate manner. Although it is customary to regard the gestation period as terminated at birth, I suggest that this is quite as erroneous a view as that which regards the life of the individual as beginning at birth. Birth is no more the beginning of the life of the individual than it is the end of gestation; it is merely the bridge between gestation within the womb and gestation continued outside the womb. It may be calendrically useful to divide up these periods as we have traditionally done, but it would appear to be quite unbiological to do so. This is unbiological because, by making such arbitrary divisions, we lose sight of the essential fact that the human infant is quite as immature at birth as is the little marsupial immaturely born into its mother's pouch, there to undergo its exterogestation until it is sufficiently matured. The human infant remains immature much longer than the infant kangaroo or opossum, but whereas the marsupial infant enjoys the protection of its mother's pouch during its period of immaturity, the human infant is afforded no such natural advantage. This is all the more reason why the parental generation in such a species must clearly understand what the immaturity of its infants really means: namely, that with all the modifications initiated by the birth process, the baby is still continuing its gestation period, passing by means of birth from uterogestation to postnatal exterogestation. The biological unity, the symbiotic relationship, maintained by mother and conceptus throughout pregnancy does not cease at birth but becomes—indeed, is naturally designed to become—even more intensive and interoperative after birth than during uterogestation. It is not simply the infant who has a great need of continuing support from its mother after birth, but that the mother has, in a complementary manner, an equally great need to continue to support and to give succor to the child. Giving birth to her child, the mother's interest is deepened and reinforced in its welfare. Her whole organism has been readied to minister to its needs, to nurse it at the breast. In nursing, the infant ingests the beneficial colostrum, but nursing also confers benefits upon the mother. The psychophysiological benefits, which in the continuing symbiotic relationship mother and child reciprocally confer upon one another, are vitally important for their future development. The transfer of maternal antibodies to the baby through the milk in breastfeeding during the early exterogestative period, thus conferring immunities upon the infant, underscores both the biological reality and importance of the symbiotic dependence of the infant upon the mother.

These facts are only slowly coming to be recognized in our highly sophisticated, mechanized, Western world, a world in which breastfeeding is considered to be something that (as one expensively educated young woman remarked to me) "only animals do," and in which there are pediatricians who assure mothers that a bottle formula is every bit as good as, and even better than, breastfeeding. We live in the logical denouement of the Machine Age, when not only are things made by machine, but human beings are turned out to be as machine-like as we can make them. We therefore see little wrong in dealing with others in a mechanical manner, since this is an age in which it is considered a mark of progress that whatever was formerly done by human beings is taken out of their hands and done by machine. It is esteemed an advance when a bottle formula can be substituted for the product of the human breast, especially in the United States, and especially in a period when many women misguidedly want to be as much like men as they are capable of becoming.

When mother and child most need each other, they are too often separated from each other, the one isolated in her room, the other banished to a crib in the nursery (so-called, presumably, because nursing is the one thing that is not done there). The separation begins from the moment of birth, so profound has our misunderstanding of the needs of human beings grown.

Perhaps the hypothesis of uterogestation and exterogestation proposed here may cause us to reconsider the meaning of the human infant's immaturity and dependency.

REFERENCES

BOSTOCK, J. Exterior Gestation, Primitive Sleep, Enuresis and Asthma: Study in Aetiology. *Med. J. Aust.* 2:149–153 (Aug. 2), 185–188 (Aug. 9) 1958.

MONTAGU, A. *Prenatal Influences.* Springfield, Ill.: Charles C Thomas Publisher, 1962.

4 It is often asserted that were equal opportunities afforded everyone, the great differences in achievement which exist between human beings would be greatly reduced. When we ask ourselves what we mean by "equal opportunities" we generally think of equal social, economic, and schooling opportunities. But as I endeavor to show in the following contribution, there is more to "equal opportunity" than that, and it is, I think, important for us to understand what that "more" is. To make that clear is the purpose of the following contribution.

And we are in need of yet another clarification. It is probably inaccurate to think that with the advent of equal opportunity, even in the sense in which I describe it, that the differences in achievement between human beings will be greatly reduced. On the contrary, I believe that they will be greatly increased, since greater opportunities will maximize the opportunities for expression of the uniqueness of each individual. It is a mistake to want to reduce differences, and a sound and humane principle to encourage the fullest expression of difference. The truth is that inequality of potentialities is the rule among humans, and that in this fact lies the great wealth of humanity; for had we all been born equal in our potentialities for achievement this would have been a very dreary world, indeed. It is because we are born with potentialities so different that we have been able to create so variegated a world.

It is, therefore, desirable for us to understand that there is nothing so unequal as the equal treatment of unequals. It is wrongheaded and even cruel to treat all human beings, especially developing human beings, as if they were equal in potentialities for learning, intelligence, and achievement. In any population taken at random there exist immense differences among individuals in rates of growth and development and in the ability to absorb what is being taught. It is as unfair to teach slow developers rapidly as it is to teach rapid developers slowly.

Each child requires to be taught as a unique individual, with special attention to his own unique rates of growth and development. And this is what we really mean when we say that human beings are born equal: that is, they are born with

"Just What Is 'Equal Opportunity'?" by Ashley Montagu. From *Vista*, 6, no. 2 (November–December 1970), 23–25, 56. Copyright © 1970 by the United Nations Association of the U.S.A. Reprinted by permission of the publisher.

equal rights to growth and development of their potentialities, with equal rights to fulfillment. "Equal rights" does not mean that every child shall be treated as if he were no different from any other child. Rather, it means that every child has a right to the recognition of his own uniqueness and individuality.

JUST WHAT IS "EQUAL OPPORTUNITY"?

Ashley Montagu

In a period when equality of opportunity is a principle which is at long last coming to be widely accepted, it is more than ever necessary to be alerted to certain problems which are bound to develop and which are likely to be with us for some time. Black children, and the children of Puerto Rican, Mexican and American Indian descent, as well as others, will increasingly continue to find themselves in schools and in other situations in which they will not, on the whole, do as well as white children. Nor, on the whole, will members of these ethnic groups do as well in the open competitive market as whites.

In schools and colleges the trend will continue for some time yet among these non-white groups, though to a lesser extent than formerly, to lag substantially behind in I.Q. tests and in school performance, as well as in general achievement.

In view of these probabilities it is desirable for everyone concerned to understand what that lag almost certainly means, in order to guard against the danger of drawing the wrong conclusions.

Observe, it will be said by many, they (especially blacks) now enjoy equal opportunities for education, and after years of it, where are their great scientists, their great inventors, their great abstract thinkers? A few writers, yes. Some athletes, yes. But, then, there has always been a sprinkling of those.

Does not this lack of achievement, under conditions of equal opportunity, fully and at long last, remove all doubt that these people are of genetically inferior stuff compared to whites?

The answer is that while it might seem so, the probabilities are that the failure to achieve equally under conditions of "equal opportunity" is due to environmental rather than to genetic deficiencies. For this conclusion there exists a considerable amount of evidence, some of which we shall consider in what follows. It is, however, much easier to attribute differences in achievement, especially scholastic achievement, to differences in innate factors, to heredity. But since the heredity of the individual represents the expression of the interaction between his genes and the environment in which those genes have undergone development, clearly the environment must always be considered as a major factor in attempting to assess the influences that have been operative in the expression of any trait. The meaning of this statement does not appear to have been always understood by those who have drawn the "obvious conclusions."

There is good reason to believe that what most of us have regarded as "equal opportunities," that is, the process of providing the young of different ethnic groups with the same conditions for learning and intellectual development have, in fact, never existed. Never existed for the simple reason that those opportunities are unequally received. The unequal reception, the evidence suggests, is due not to group genetic differences, but to group cultural differences, to culturally produced impediments in the ability to learn and to think in comparatively similar ways of abstraction.

For high, even adequate, intellectual achievement certain prerequisite conditions are apparently necessary, quite unrelated to the quality of the genetic potentialities of the individual, assuming, of course, that those potentialities are normal. The necessary conditions are complex, but may be described as a stimulating cultural environment which encourages high aspiration levels.

A black child from the ghetto in the same classroom with a white child from the neighboring white slum area is not enjoying equal opportunities in the classroom for the simple reason that he is not in a position to learn as relevant to himself much to which he is being exposed. The school generally offers him little that he can creatively incorporate into the background of his own ghetto culture. . . .

It is not sufficiently often pointed out that every individual must learn to learn, and that a great part of this is accomplished by the kind of stimulation he receives in the home, in relationships with parents and siblings, long before the child gets to school. The child, other things being more or less equal, will learn in the school in a manner very largely influenced by the kind of learning experiences he has undergone at home. Here the white child enjoys immense advantages over the black. By the time the black child arrives at school he has usually suffered massive deprivations which have resulted not only in a serious failure of development in his learning capacities, but also in his ability to assimilate what he does learn in anything like the meaningful context and manner with which the white child is able to learn.

The kind of changes that must occur in the black home and culture before the black child can enter the classroom on an equal footing with, and as prepared to learn as, the white child are complex. These changes probably belong in the same category as those that are and have been operative in many societies in which peoples of very different cultural backgrounds have come together without the more highly developed one, after many centuries, seeming to have any significant effect in stimulating the creativity of the acculturated group.

Let me give some examples of this.

The Romans occupied Britain for five hundred years, but insofar as any possible stimulus to creativity was concerned the Britons seem largely to have escaped it. Invasions by Scandinavians, Celts, Angles, Jutes, Saxons and Normans, extending over a period of more than a thousand years, similarly seem to have had little effect. It would, indeed, have been easy to conclude that the Britons were a genetically ill-endowed people. Following all that contact and stimulation by so many different peoples what did the native population have to show for it? An Adam Bede, a Roger Bacon, and the author of *Everyman*? It wasn't much.

And then, all of a sudden, as it were, in the sixteenth century, there was such an explosion of bright stars as the world had not witnessed since the days of Periclean Athens. The appearance of so many major constellations that so unexpectedly illuminated the hitherto virtually empty English firmament: Shakespeare, John

Donne, Thomas Heywood, George Chapman, Ben Jonson, Thomas Dekker, Philip Massinger, Christopher Marlowe, Francis Bacon, Gilbert of Colchester, as well as numerous other luminous spirits who followed in a continuous succession of new stellar births, would have been considered highly improbable by most of Britain's conquerors.

It is of interest to note that all these men, including the philosophers and scientists among them, were individuals of outstanding imaginative genius. It was during the second half of the following century, the seventeenth, that there was to develop that equally striking florescence of scientific genius.

From the Roman occupation to the appearance of the first men of genius and high achievement it took fifteen hundred years. This is, of course, a very crass and incomplete statement. A good deal of simmering had undoubtedly gone on for some centuries prior to what appears to have been a sudden explosion of genius. Nevertheless, the fact remains that it was only after fifteen hundred years of acculturative interaction, or whatever it was that was involved, that the English began popping.

It is to be observed that we are speaking here of "high achievement," of "genius." It is by the works of such individuals that we customarily evaluate a society's or an ethnic group's quality. Apparently certain specific conditions must develop in every culture before the latent potentialities for achievement in each population can be expressed.

What are these necessary specific conditions? These conditions are no longer a matter of conjecture, but on the basis of increasing evidence may be dependably deduced and indicated. The conditions necessary for achievement in any society are:

1. A cultural background of respect for achievement in the family in which the child has been raised.
2. Encouragements and rewards within the family and the culture which make it possible for the individual to acquire whatever is necessary in order for him to achieve in an achieving society.
3. A society in which the conditions of individual development have not physically affected his ability to learn. Nutritional deficiencies, for example, during fetal development may irreversibly damage large numbers of brain cells, and thus seriously affect the child's ability to learn. Nutri-

tional deficiencies during infancy or childhood may produce similar damaging effects.

The effects of some diseases during the early stages of development, prenatal and postnatal, can be equally damaging.

Nutritional deficiencies, especially protein deficiencies, as well as deficiencies induced by disease, are widespread throughout the world, and probably affected whole populations throughout the prehistoric period. This may, at least in part, account for the slow rate of cultural development during the greater portion of man's more than five million years of evolution. During that long period of secular time the struggle to survive probably involved durable periods of undernourishment. There may have been prolonged periods when man suffered from protein and vitamin deficiencies, especially ascorbemia, that is, vitamin-C deficiency, a natural deficiency since man lacks the ability to produce it within his own body and must acquire it mainly from fruits of the citrus variety.

The combination of these factors: (1), the continuous and demanding struggle for existence, (2), the debilitating effects of disease, (3), the occasionally damaging effects of malnutrition, would severely limit the members of any population from achieving very much more than was necessary for bare survival. Add to this combination of factors those which continue to exist for many contemporary populations, . . . (4), lack of encouragements, rewards, incentives, motivations, and aspirations for extraordinary achievement, and we have the necessary and sufficient conditions for ensuring the nondevelopment of any and all potentialities for extraordinary or even ordinary accomplishment.

Potentialities require the proper environing conditions if they are to grow and develop and find appropriate expression. The expression of any capacity requires opportunities which stimulate the capacities to develop into abilities. Human development is not simply a matter of the unfolding of genetic potentialities but principally a matter of the cumulative, active process of utilizing environmental inputs. The adequate utilization of those inputs depends upon the environmental opportunities afforded the utilizing mechanisms, that is, the genetic potentials. The joker in that pack is, of course, the word "opportunities."

What are "opportunities"? What most culturally developed peoples with masses of nondeveloped people living in their midst have interpreted "opportunities" to mean is the hypocritically simplistic notion that political, legal and educational rights somehow ensure the freedom to enjoy equal rights in everything else. This is, of course, utter nonsense. The laws on the books assuring equal political, legal and educational rights to all citizens are, in practice, differentially applied and enforced. Equal laws do not in practice work out either as equality before the law or equality of opportunity. Prejudice and discrimination operate to maintain impassable barriers against the subclasses who, as I pointed out many years ago, are treated as members of a lower caste.

In the deprived and depressed conditions under which the members of subclasses or castes are forced to live they are deprived of the greatest of all opportunities: *the opportunity to learn to respond with advantage to available opportunities*. The absence of this basic opportunity, by whatever means produced, seriously interferes with the ability to respond to the available opportunities.

The *basic opportunity* necessary for all human beings if they are to realize their potentialities is comprised of the obverse of those factors which I have described as principally responsible for the lack of high achievement in the members of certain populations. The necessary ingredients in *basic opportunity* then, necessary for achievement, are:

1. Some freedom from the continuous pressure to survive, that is, the enjoyment of a certain amount of leisure.
2. Good health or relative freedom from disease during fetal and childhood development.
3. Freedom from the effects of malnutrition during fetal, childhood and adult development.
4. Growth and development in an environment with traditional roots in a cultural background providing the matrix and the context from and in which are derived those meanings which, in terms of those meanings, make the world intelligible and meaningful to the child and the person he becomes. If the traditional roots are deep and extensive, and his cultural background rich and multidimensional, he will have within him what used to be called "an apperceptive mass" which will enable him to respond with advantage to the environment in which he finds himself. If, on the other hand, his traditional roots are shallow or non-

existent and his cultural background arid, he will himself be unable to take root and develop in what remains an essentially inhospitable environment.

5. Finally, for creativity and achievement the encouragement and nurturing of high aspiration levels, the fueling and development of incentives, the promise and experience of rewards are necessary.

Genius or high achievement remains an unexpressed potentiality in the absence of these conditions. In order to start its motors running not only is the fuel necessary, the opportunities, but the fuel must be ignited, and that is accomplished not merely by turning the key in the ignition, but by ensuring the presence of an adequately charged battery, *the basic opportunity.* A healthy battery, adequately charged, properly connected to the spark plugs, will respond to the key being turned in the ignition, but not otherwise. All the necessary conditions must be fulfilled if the engine is to be started and to be kept running. It matters not how otherwise well we attend to the design of the car, it will not run unless the basic requirements of its motor are met. So it is with human beings. Unless the basic internal requirements for achievement are met, no matter what external opportunities they are exposed to, they will largely be unable to respond to them. The process of achievement is a creative one, creating power by a complex of relations, which are only made possible in an environment of *basic opportunity.*

Most of us are not persons of great or extraordinary achievement, and it is desirable to recognize that in every human context it is not genius in some specific area that is of significance, but rather the generalized ability to make the appropriately successful responses to the ordinary challenges presented by the environment, to be plastic, malleable, and adaptable. And of such adaptive behavior all men everywhere, within the normal range of variation, are capable. Nevertheless, we tend to evaluate the status of societies by the measure of their extraordinary accomplishments. This is fair enough, but it is quite unfair to draw the conclusion from the differences in accomplishment that those which have fewer accomplishments to their credit than others are therefore genetically inferior to the others.

By this measure the Britons would have been held genetically inferior to the Romans. But the truth is they were *not* genetically inferior, but only culturally different, and apparently for the most part quite unmotivated for the very good reason that the conditions of life were such as to be all time-consuming in the struggle for survival. Basic opportunities were almost completely wanting, and it was not until such opportunities were afforded an increasingly large number of individuals in the population that a Shakespeare could make his appearance.

Until similar basic opportunities are afforded all populations compared, whether they be the aborigines of New Guinea or the blacks of New York, it were premature as well as wholly unjustifiable to attribute differences in achievement between populations to genetic factors.

It is, apparently, difficult to persuade those who are so ready to settle for a genetic explanation of differences in cultural achievement that it is only by equalizing basic opportunities for everyone that the conditions will be provided for making any sort of valid judgments concerning the possible role played by genetic factors in social and individual differences in cultural achievement. Until such basic opportunities are made available to everyone, all statements attributing differences in cultural achievement must be adjudged what they are: conjectures without any scientific basis or merit whatever.

Ultimately, of course, the whole question of "race" is a pseudo one, a system of pseudological rationalizations based on insufficiently analyzed evidence designed, usually, to bolster prejudices and defend indefensible positions, and which at once denies and rejects science, logic and humanity. However unsound and unreal such beliefs may be, we know only too well how very real the unsound and the unreal can become. Be that as it may, it cannot be too often repeated that the issue at stake is not a scientific one, but a question of ethics. By virtue of the fact that he is a human being every individual has a right to his birthright, which is development. The greatest riches of the person, of his community, of humanity, lies in the uniqueness of the contribution that each individual has to make to his fellowman.

It is not a question of "superiority" or "inferiority" but the encouragement of individual fulfillment, whatever the individual's limitations, that society must consider among the first of the purposes for which it exists. The greatest of all talents, and the most important for man, is the talent for humanity. And what is talent? It is involvement. And the talent for being humane operationally means the involvement in the welfare of one's fellowman. All human beings have the capacity for such involvement. Racists commit the greatest of all crimes because they obstruct the development of this capacity and prevent the individual's fulfillment as a human being. To the extent that these crimes are committed, to that extent is the individual, society and humanity impoverished.

The deprivation of any man's right to fulfillment diminishes each of us, for we, as well as he, have lost what he has been deprived of, for we are all involved in each other. Whether we wish it to be so or not this involvement is inherent in the very nature of nature, and especially of human nature. The most basic of all opportunities is the right to growth and development as a humane being who has been deeply involved in the love of others, for the health and identity of the person consists in the meaningfulness of his interrelationships.

5 It was explained in a preceding article, "The Origin and Significance of Neonatal and Infant Immaturity in Man," that in the first years of a child's life, his brain grows at a remarkable rate. This growth entails the forming of connections between nerve cells within the brain, thus enabling messages to be sent from the brain to the muscles, telling them how to move; from the skin and the inner organs to the brain, giving it information about feelings; and from one part of the brain to another, making possible the integration of different kinds of information and consequently such human qualities of mind as language, visual imagery, verbalizable emotion, and so on. These neural pathways are not formed automatically; rather, they develop as a result of experience which provides input and therefore stimulation to the brain's growth.

Sociogenic brain damage refers to damage done to the maturation of the brain by depriving it of the social stimulation necessary for the development of those neural interrelations essential for successful mental functioning. By "successful" I here mean the ability to make the appropriately successful responses to the challenges of the social environment. It should be emphasized that by "damage" I do not mean that any nervous tissues are destroyed, but rather that normal growth and development of neural connections fails to occur in the absence of the necessary developmental stimuli. Just as in physical malnutrition nerve cells fail to grow and develop properly, so also in social malnutrition, where the physical nutrition may be quite satisfactory, there is a similar failure of neural growth and development. We now have a good deal of experimental evidence on other animals and on the effects of physical malnutrition on the brain of both other animals and humans which strongly suggests that sociogenic brain damage is as real a phenomenon in humans as it is in animals.

In the contribution which follows, the evidence is discussed of conditions which frequently lead to sociogenic brain damage, especially in such a markedly socially stratified society as that of the United States. In addition, there is discussion of the practical implications for the better understanding and more significant handling of these conditions. It is hoped that the reader will be stimulated to think about the implications

"Sociogenic Brain Damage" by Ashley Montagu. Reprinted from the *American Anthropologist*, 74, no. 5 (October 1972), 1045–61.

this information has for his own individual and social conduct.

The relation between culture and human development here becomes especially significant when it is understood what a deleterious effect upon the physical basis of mind an impoverished cultural environment is capable of having.

It should not, however, be assumed that sociogenic brain damage is irreversible. The probabilities are high, in humans at least, that the damage is reversible. What sociogenic brain damage does is to make it much more difficult for the child so affected to learn and to keep up with unaffected children, especially in the learning environment of the school.

SOCIOGENIC BRAIN DAMAGE

Ashley Montagu

Sociogenic brain damage is a condition produced by impoverished social environments. This has been demonstrated conclusively in rats. It is very probable that similar damage from similar causes is produced in the brains of infants, children, and even adolescents. The damage is probably akin to that which is produced by physical malnutrition. There is reason to believe that poverty and the ghetto, often associated with both physical and social malnutrition, constitute a combination of conditions capable of producing severe failures in neural development with its attendant failures in learning ability. The focus on sociogenic brain damage as alone capable of producing such learning deficits is related in this paper to the question of what so-called IQ tests really measure.

When the functions of the brain are disordered in neuromuscular, structural, chemical, electrical, or other observable ways, the tendency has been to look for the organic causes of the disorder or malformation. Function is the other face of structure. Functions are dependent upon organic structures, hence, the obvious, though not necessarily accurate conclusion is customarily drawn that disordered function must be caused by disordered structures, and frequently we tend to look no further. We tend, in our thinking, to be limited to the idea that physical factors such as genetic, viral, bacterial, parasitic, chemical, iatrogenic, complications of pregnancy, prematurity, postmaturity, and the like are the kind of factors that must be involved in the brain damage that causes the observable malfunction. This is often quite true, but it is also quite frequently not the whole story. No more the whole story than that pellagra is due to a deficiency of vitamins of the B complex, especially niacin (nicotinic acid) and its amide. It is quite true that under any conditions a diet deficient in nicotinic acid and other vitamins of the B complex will result in pellagra. In fact, however, under ordinary normal socio-economic conditions the diet is likely to be more than adequate in B complex vitamins. Hence, the question must be asked whether or not the socio-economic conditions in most cases constitute the principal factor in the causation of pellagra? Ever since 1915, we have known, thanks to the work of Goldberger, that pellagra is a disorder of extreme poverty, most unlikely to occur among those who can afford an adequate diet.

While it should be obvious that no matter how inadequate the socio-economic conditions may be, if the diet is adequate, pellagra will not develop, nevertheless, it is almost exclusively under poor socio-economic conditions that pellagra is most often encountered. In 1917–18 there were over 200,000 cases of pellagra in the United States, and deaths from the condition numbered 10,000 annually. Between 1929 and 1949 the decrease in mortality in the southern states, where pellagra most frequently occurred, was striking: from 22.4 to 5.1 per 100,000. The number of acute cases and deaths from this disorder is today very low, largely as the result of a limited improvement in the dietary intake of people living in socio-economically depressed environments. So it was not really the deficiency in niacin intake that was the principal cause of pellagra, but a socio-economic environment which led to that deficiency.

Indeed, it would appear that many, if not most, disorders are to a significant extent due to social conditions resulting from an environment impoverished in the elements necessary for the maintenance of health.

There is a class of brain damage of sociogenic origin to which, it seems to me, insufficient attention has been paid. Functional expressions of this class of brain damage are the deficits in behavior, and especially in motivation, learning ability, and intelligence which are produced by malnutrition.

It is generally agreed that the most important factor in the healthy development of the conceptus is nutrition—not merely the nutrition derived from the mother, but also the nutrition of the mother's mother, and probably also of the mother's father, not to mention the child's own father (Montagu 1962).

At twenty weeks fetal age to thirty weeks fetal age in the human female there are about seven million oocytes present in the ovary which, by about forty weeks fetal age become enveloped by granulosa cells, forming follicles containing ova which are already in the prophase of meiotic division. During later fetal life and childhood, these follicles undergo successive waves of development and atresia, the number of primordial follicles falling from a maximum of two million just before birth to about 300,000 in the adult (Kase 1969). Should the fetus suffer from inadequate nutrition, these egg-cells, like all tissues of the fetus, may be detrimentally affected. The process of mitosis, from interphase, through prophase, metaphase, anaphase, to telophase, takes about eighteen hours, and meiosis almost as long (Swanson 1964). During those fundamental phases of genetic development, almost anything can happen to the cellular structures as a consequence of inadequate nutrition. Not alone the female, but the male who has himself suffered from malnutrition during his postnatal life may also have suffered some damage to his gonadal tissues. These are not conjectures. We know them to be very real possibilities. For a detailed discussion of the effects of malnutrition upon offspring, reference may be made to the excellent book on disadvantaged children by Herbert G. Birch and Joan Dye Gussow (1969). Morbidity, mortality, and teratogenic rates are significantly higher in the children of malnourished pregnant women than in those who were adequately nourished. Height, weight, and intelligence are also lower in the children of malnourished mothers. These are important facts, and they have long been known, even though the relation of fetal and childhood malnutrition to lowered intelligence does not seem to have stirred those who should have been most impressed by it. The physicalistic or biogenic bias seems to have been largely responsible for the failure to recognize the role played by social conditions in the causation of physical and behavioral deficiencies.

Maternal malnutrition in relation to impairment of the offspring has received some attention, but the role of paternal malnutrition in producing deficits in his offspring has been largely neglected. Stieve has shown, both in other animals and in man, that malnutrition may severely injure the sexual tissues in both male and female. Stieve found that stressful conditions of any kind may damage the development of sperm, and that such sperm fertilizing a normal ovum may jeopardize the healthy development of the conceptus. Stieve also found that at the very moment the female undergoes a stressful experience "and there is in the ovary a follicle ready to emerge or almost so, it does not erupt, but instead collapses and the whole follicle degenerates" (Stieve 1942, 1949, 1951; Iagrashi et al. 1965). Stress in the mother may have a more or less damaging effect upon the ovary as a whole or upon specific ova in it. Selye and others have produced abundant evidence that in rats the characteristic response of the female sex organs to systemic stress manifests itself mainly by ovarian atrophy and more or less permanent suppression of the female sex cycle (anestrus) (Selye 1950). Physiologically these changes are known to be due to decreased gonadotrophin production from the anterior lobe of the pituitary. It is highly probable that a similar mechanism, under similar conditions, is at work in the human female (Gantt 1950; Taylor 1950). To malnutrition, and as a factor entirely apart from it, resulting from the pressures of a disadvantaged socio-economic environment must be added stress. It is known that stress alone is capable of exerting all sorts of unfavorable effects upon the developing conceptus and child. Interaction of stress with the genotype is discussed in Joffe's book *Prenatal Determinants of Behaviour* (1969) and in my own book *Prenatal Influences* (1962). Stott, in his book *Studies of Troublesome Children* (1966), has stated the case for prenatal neural damage to the fetus of the stressed pregnant mother. The harm may vary from actual damage to brain tissue to abnormalities of metabolism impinging on brain tissue. Göllnitz has proposed a syndromic axis with the milder forms including over-reactivity, distractibility, stimulus domination, variability of mood, of motivation, and of bodily function, and general behavior disturbance. The more severe forms comprise emotional explosiveness, rage responses, passivity, loss of insight, slowing up of thought processes, and general personality disintegration (Göllnitz 1963–64). Birch speaks of brain damage as referring to a behavior syndrome and not to the fact of brain damage as such (1964) and this may well apply to dysfunctional behavior resulting from temporary impairments of brain function, such as the conditions he describes, namely, developmental lag, behavior disturbance, motor awkwardness, minor perceptual disturbance, and distractibility; to which malfunctions Stott would add a number of symptoms indicative of inefficient neural control or regulation of the soma: poor vocal articulation, faults of homeostasis, enuresis, excessive sweating or salivation, choroid movements, restless or over-heavy sleep, "hysterical" pains and disabilities (1966).

It would be quite misleading to suggest that we understand the nature of the morphological or metabolic counterparts of these phenomena. We do not. In the absence of firm evidence of brain damage in behavioral impairments or disorders, the inference can at best be presumptive only. Stott (1966) therefore suggests that we use the less tendentious term neural impairment or neural dysfunction in preference to brain damage. The suggestion has merit for some of the less severe deficits or impairments to which Stott refers and which were characteristic of his disadvantaged troublesome children. My purpose, however, here is to suggest that there exists a whole range of behavioral deficits due to brain damage which is rather more subtle, and which is sociogenic in origin. Hence, while agreeing with Stott that neural impairment or dysfunction may be a better term for the milder forms of behavioral disorders he has considered, I shall here be discussing the disorders which I believe are due to sociogenic brain damage.

EARLY MALNOURISHMENT

There is a universal embryogenic law to the effect that the earlier the noxious influences to which the organism is exposed the more severe is the developmental damage. This law extends to the whole developmental period, and especially to the earlier stages of prenatal development. The living organism is so sensitive that even after it has achieved growth and development, unfavorable environmental influences may severely adversely affect the organism at any time during later life. This was tragically demonstrated by what happened to many concentration-camp victims of the Nazis during World War II. For example, among a group of Norwegians who had been prisoners of the Nazis, those who had been in the concentration camps the longest, and had suffered the severest deprivations and abuses, presented the most serious evidence of impairment of brain function and structure. "Late sequelae of the suffering and misery," writes Wolff, "were major behavior disturbances and even degenerative changes in the brain. . . . Defects were roughly proportional to the duration and intensity of the abuse" (Wolff 1968:209). Such were the effects of stress upon fully developed adults. It would hardly be a bold speculation to suggest that similar stresses may be transmitted, in humoral and metabolic forms, through the placenta to the tissues of the developing conceptus and especially to the brain. Man's total number of brain cells, thirteen billion, appears to be established by twenty-five fetal weeks of age. On experimental animals, the evidence indicates that behavior disturbances as a consequence of damaging environmental effects may be irreversible (Bronfenbrenner 1968). There is good evidence that chromosomal structure may be so affected, even to the extent of disturbing chromosomal mechanisms and resulting in such disorders as Down's syndrome (Drillien and Wilkinson 1964; Montagu 1962; Stott 1961). Recent research indicates that behavior may be seriously affected as a result of metabolic disturbances in the monoamines of the brain, the catecholamines, norepinephrine and dopamine, and the indole amine, serotonin, acting differentially in the different parts of the brain in which they are mostly found (Schildkraut and Kety 1967).

That socio-economic environmental factors may determine the conditions which directly affect the very elements which influence the constitutional development of the individual, long before that individual is even conceived, and substantively after conception, is now no longer disputable.

In the fourteen largest cities of the United States in 1950, approximately one child out of ten was culturally underprivileged or deprived. By 1960, this figure had risen to one in three (Reissman 1962). In 1970, this figure approached almost one in two enrolled in the public schools of these large cities (Reissman 1962). In the Santiago slums, in Chile, Dr. Fernando Mönckeberg found that forty-five percent of the preschool children were mentally deficient while between sixty and seventy percent of the children were malnourished (Mönckeberg 1968, 1970). There can be very little doubt that much the same conditions prevail in the slums of other impoverished regions virtually everywhere in the Americas. Throughout the Americas there is a high positive correlation between poor socio-economic conditions and malnutrition. Low per capita income, illiteracy, low cultural level, bad sanitary conditions, low intellectual performance of the underprivileged groups, and finally, racial and religious prejudices. Faced as we are with a coming world situation in which there will be less and less food for more and more people, a world in which the complexities of the social and political conditions thus exacerbated will render even more difficult the problems which will confront us, the challenge presented to us becomes urgently more pressing each hour, and with each hour the time grows short.

It has been conservatively estimated that the total number of malnourished children in the world between the ages of one and six years reached 269 million in 1966, 276 million in 1967, 329 million in 1968 (May and Lemons 1969), well over 400 million in 1969, and well over 460 million in 1970. By the end of this century, when world population is expected to double to over seven billion, it is more than likely, if present trends continue, that there will be more than a billion malnourished children on this earth, and that eighty percent of all inhabitants will be living in those parts of the world in which hunger is now a predominant everyday fact of life.

Dr. Mönckeberg's findings in Santiago present a shocking example of conditions that are not only widespread throughout the Americas, but are also reported from many other parts of the world (György and Kline 1970). Furthermore, those findings present something of a forecast of the shape of things to come should we fail to take the proper measures in time. Hence, it is important to set out Dr. Mönckeberg's findings, and to reflect upon their meaning.

Dr. Mönckeberg found that only fifty-one percent of his malnourished preschool children had a normal development quotient of over 85. The percentage of adequately nourished children rated as normal from the slums, ninety-five percent, was very similar, ninety-seven percent, for the children from middle class homes in Santiago.

In 150 preschool children from a very low class homogeneous population in which malnutrition was prevalent, Dr. Mönckeberg found a marked difference in intellectual capacity in children whose weights were under the third percentile on a standard scale and had a marked growth retardation, as compared with those children whose weights were over the tenth percentile and were considered nutritionally normal. A very significant relationship was found between the degree of growth retardation, when outside the normal limits, and psychomotor development.

In addition to growth retardation, these children had smaller heads than those of 500 adequately nourished middle class children. These deficits in cranial growth were significantly correlated with decreased IQ. In infants with severe marasmus during the first months of life, not only is the head smaller, but the brain is disproportionately smaller than the head. In normal children, transillumination of the skull with a beam from a 500 watt bulb directed at the top of the head will show a zone of illumination approximately two centimeters wide around the point of contact between the light and the child's head. In children with marasmus, a much larger portion of the skull is illuminated, and in many cases, the entire skull, thus dramatically indicating the massive retardation of brain growth in these children.

In order to determine whether the early effects of malnutrition could be reversed, Dr. Mönckeberg conducted a follow-up study on fourteen children admitted to a hospital with severe malnutrition beginning during the first months of life. Following long periods of treatment in the hospital, the children continued to make outpatient visits and received twenty liters of free milk per month. At three to six years of age, the clinical appearance and biochemical index of these children appear to be normal. Weight is within normal limits, but the children are short for their age. Head circumference is below normal, and the average IQ is only 62, significantly below the average of Chilean preschool children from low socioeconomic areas. In no case was a child's IQ above 76. Since it is well established that brain growth, consisting largely of protein synthesis, takes place early in the life of the child, Dr. Mönckeberg concluded "it is logical to assume that the effects of malnutrition during this critical period are permanent" (1968:30–31).

Cravioto, summarizing the results of many studies on the relation of malnutrition to development, concludes "that the existence of an association between protein-calorie malnutrition in infancy and retardation in mental development has been established beyond reasonable doubt. It can also be stated that there is a high probability that this lag in mental development may have long lasting consequences if severe malnutrition is experienced at a very early age in the life of the child" (1970:12). In a similar survey, Eichenwald and Fry conclude, "Observations on animals and human infants suggest that malnutrition during a critical period of early life results in short stature and may, in addition, permanently and profoundly affect the future intellectual and emotional development of the individual" (1969:648).

Since in malnutrition it would be expected that the lack of adequate protein and the vitamin and calorie deficiencies which are so often its accompaniments would affect the DNA and RNA which directs the formation of proteins, this has recently become the subject of inquiry. Winick and Rosso determined the amount of DNA in the brains of children who died of malnutrition as compared with the amount in the brains of normally nourished children. They found the amount of DNA in the brains of the malnourished children to be significantly less, thus indicating the presence of a substantially smaller number of brain cells. Head circumference, brain weight, and protein content, were all reduced (Winick 1968, 1970; Winick and Rosso 1969a, 1969b). The protein-vitamin-calorie deficiencies may so affect DNA or RNA or both so that the mechanisms for incorporating amino acids into body proteins either cease to operate fully or function in abnormal ways.

Zamenhof and his co-workers have shown that deficient diets administered to female rats before and during pregnancy result in offspring that exhibit a substantial reduction in total brain DNA, and hence, presumably, in a reduction in the total number of brain cells. Such offspring also show behavioral deficiencies (1968, 1971).

Myelination, cellular differentiation, development of arborizing collaterals between neurones (Dobbing 1964, 1968, 1970a, 1970b; Schapiro and Vukovich 1970; Sterman et al. 1971; Davison and Dobbing 1968), and chemical structure of the nervous system (Bass, Netsky, and Young 1970a, 1970b) may all be seriously affected in the malnourished child with more or less serious consequences for its ability to learn or develop into a normally competent human being (Hurley 1969; Osler and Cooke 1965; Grotberg 1969; Deutsch et al. 1967).

Stress factors of every sort are of the very essence of the life of the poor: physical illness, broken homes, malnutrition, emotional strain, and almost every kind of social deprivation. Every investigation that has ever been conducted on this subject has agreed in finding that poverty is the principal cause of most of the developmental retardation encountered in human beings (Sanders 1934; Hunt 1969).

Social Deprivation

Let us now turn our attention to a direct retardative influence on the development of the brain which is entirely the result of unfavorable social conditions. It has been known for many years that health, intelligence, achievement, and socially adequate behavior are highly correlated with socio-economic factors: the better the socio-economic environment the higher the scores achieved on all these parameters (Lesser et al. 1965). But more than that, the evidence is clear that the growth and development of the nervous system and the sense organs is greatly influenced by the social experience of the organism. One of the earliest, and now classical, experimental demonstrations of the effect of environmental experience on the development of the nervous system was George Ellett Coghill's investigation of the development of the salamander *Amblystoma punctatum*, set out in many papers and in his classic book *Anatomy and the Problem of Behaviour* (Coghill 1929). Coghill showed that neuronal development was markedly more developed in stimulated than in nonstimulated animals. Axon terminals and the growth of collaterals was much more active in the stimulated than in the non-stimulated animals. Coghill concluded his book with the memorable words, "The real measure of the individual . . . whether lower animal or man, must include the element of growth as a creative power.

Man is, indeed, a mechanism, but he is a mechanism which, within the limitations of life, sensitivity and growth, is creating and operating himself" (1929:110). The individual deprived of the stimulations necessary for the development of sensitivity and growth simply fails to develop in these modalities, and in the ability to create and operate himself (Ambrose 1969; Michael 1968; Tobach, Aronson, and Shaw 1971). For human beings, this is the greatest of all disasters. The greatest evil and the most enduring of all tragedies for the individual and his society lies in the difference between what he was capable of becoming and what he has in fact been caused to become.

It is of such sociogenically induced tragedies that I speak here. These tragedies and the mechanism of their production are of more than clinical interest, for there have always been those among us who have been eager to claim a genetic causation for such misfortunes, and to make such presumed and unsubstantiated genetic causes the basis for social policy. This has been especially so in connection with the problem-solving form of behavior we call intelligence, especially as allegedly measured by IQ tests.

Intelligence is something which develops as the result of the interaction of brain potentials with experience, nutritional and social. Fundamentally and functionally, intelligence is both a special and general ability resulting primarily from the social organization of brain potentials for the making of adaptive responses to the particular challenges of the environment. At birth, the brain is continuing the accelerated rate of growth which began during the last two months of intrauterine development, gaining weight at the rate of between one and two milligrams a minute, a rate which is continued throughout the first six months. By the end of this period, the brain has virtually doubled in size, from a weight of 350 to 656 grams, a gain of 306 grams. The size of this increment exceeds by far anything ever achieved this way again (see Table 1). By the end of the first year, the rate of increase has decelerated to half the rate of the first six months, when the brain attains a weight of 825 grams. The same decelerated rate is maintained during the whole of the second year, with the brain achieving a weight of 1010 grams. During the third year, there is a further deceleration to one-third the rate of the first six months. And by the end of the third year, the brain of the average three-year-old has achieved more than four-fifths of its maximum

TABLE 1. GROWTH OF THE HUMAN BRAIN

Fetus Lunar Months	Weight in Grams	Gain in Grams	Percent of Gain	
5	62.5	25.5	40.0	
6	88.0	25.5	29.0	
8	277.0	189.0	68.6	A threefold increase in weight in this two-month period
9 birth	350/392	73/115	30.0	An increment of about a third the previous month's weight
½ year	656.0	306.0	47.0	Almost doubles in weight in first six months
1	825.0	169.0	20.5	Reduction to half rate of increase of first six months
2	1010.0	185.0	18.3	Reduction to half rate of increase of first six months
3	1115.0	105.0	9.4	Reduction to one-third rate of increase of first six months
4	1180.0	75.0	6.4	Gradual deceleration of rate of growth
6	1250.0	70.0	5.6	
9	1307.0	57.0	4.3	
12	1338.0	31.0	3.3	
20–29	1396.0	58.0	4.0	

adult size. At the end of the third year, the child's brain weighs, on the average, 1115 grams. When the brain attains its maximum size, at between twenty and twenty-nine years, it will have added, in the additional seventeen or so years, no more than 281 grams to the grand total of 1396 grams.

All the evidence suggests that during the long period of brain growth, and especially during the first critical three years, it is probably the first six months, when the brain is in its most rapid phase of growth and cell number is also increasing, that are the most critical.

CRITICAL PERIODS IN BRAIN DEVELOPMENT

The evidence further suggests that at birth the human neonate is only half gestated, and that he completes his gestation, like the little marsupial, outside the womb. This latter developmental period I have called *exterogestation*. It terminates when the infant begins to crawl about for himself, at about nine or ten months (Montagu 1961). The infant of humankind is much more precariously poised in relation to the environment than we have been accustomed to think. He is born biologically premature in every respect, and it is during the first six months of postnatal life that the brain, continuing its fetal rate of growth, accomplishes all that packaging of cellular materials which will serve it for the rest of its life. The whole of the first three years of postnatal life will constitute the period of the experiential, the social, organization of those nervous tissues. The early first three years of rapid brain growth coincide with the fundamental learning period of the child, of the individual. Upon learning, that is, upon the social organization of his brain, almost the whole of the individual's later integrative behavioral abilities will depend. It is during this critical period that purely social environmental deficiencies may seriously and detrimentally affect the organization of the brain.

Such deficiencies often result in what may be termed the *social deprivation syndrome*. This syndrome is principally characterized by a short attention span and learning difficulties resulting in poor test performance. This is usually measured in a lower than normal IQ test score, in poor school and poor social performance. Such deficits are commonly attributed to genetic inadequacies. The difficulty is, indeed, that the social deprivation syndrome mimics the genetically influenced condition. Such mimicked conditions are known as phenocopies; that is to say, the apparent condition resembles the genetic one, but is in fact due to nongenetic causes. Much ink has been spilled and many a reputation lost in the sinuous convolutions of this difficult subject in the endeavor by many writers to show that such behavioral deficits are principally due to genetic factors.

There can be not the least doubt that there exist many behavioral deficits of this sort that are due to genetic deficiencies (Levitan and Montagu 1971). It is, therefore, of great importance to be able to distinguish the genetic conditions from the phenocopies. We cannot, at present, do much to prevent the birth of genetically influenced poor learners, but we can do a great deal to prevent the development of poor learners who owe their disability to nothing more nor less than a poor social environment.

With rather monotonous regularity there appear, at almost predictable intervals, elaborate studies which purport to show that certain racial or ethnic or social groups of other kinds are, on the whole, poorer learners and achievers and score significantly lower on IQ tests than the group to which the investigator happens to belong. Such reports invariably suffer the same eventual fate. They are lauded by those who prefer to believe what these studies purport to demonstrate, and are severely criticized and condemned by the experts. Following a period of perfervid discussion in the press, and partisan misuse in legislatures, the brouhaha generally dies down, and the entire incident is finally consigned to the archives in which such incidents are eventually preserved. In the meantime, aid and comfort has been given to racists, segregationists, those who perhaps should know better, and serve to fortify in their citadels of infallibility the half-educated and the many who have been "educated" beyond their intelligence.

The latest work of this kind is by Arthur Jensen, Professor of Educational Psychology at the University of California, Berkeley. In a study entitled "How much can we boost IQ and scholastic achievement?" published in the Winter 1969 issue of the *Harvard Educational Review,* Jensen argues that it is "a not unreasonable hypothesis that genetic factors are strongly implicated in the average Negro-White intelligence difference" (1969:82). Jensen then proceeds to show what everyone has known since the initiation of intelligence testing, namely, that Blacks on the average do not do as well on such tests as Whites. As others have done before him, Jensen attributes this difference largely to the operation of genetic factors, believing as he does that the IQ test constitutes the best available method of measuring the genetic contribution to intelligence. As Lee Edson, an expositor of Jensen's claims, put it, intelligence, which Jensen "equates with the ability measured by IQ tests, is largely inherited, a matter of genes and brain structure, and therefore no amount of compensatory education or forced exposure to culture is going to improve it substantially" (1969:11). In brief, whatever it is that intelligence tests measure is, according to Jensen, intelligence. This is, of course, a circular statement, and therefore no definition at all. Furthermore, he holds that intelligence is largely genetically determined. It has been suggested that the only thing IQ tests really measure is the intelligence of the intelligence tester. I think there is more to be said for this suggestion than for that which proposes that IQ tests largely measure genetic intelligence, for the facts, derived from innumerable studies, indicate that what IQ tests measure is very far removed from the genetic potentials for intelligence: that what IQ tests measure represents the expression of the interaction between those genetic potentials and the nutritional, socio-economic, emotional, motivational, and schooling experience of the individual (Hunt 1961).

One wonders whether those who are so ready to settle for the genetic factor as the principal cause of the differences in IQ between Blacks and Whites would also hold that the enormous overall differences, at every age level, in morbidity and mortality rates, between these two groups are also due to genetic factors? Or that Messrs Maddox of Georgia and Wallace of Alabama are where they are because of genetic factors, while no Black has ever occupied a similar office in those states for similar genetic reasons? Whatever their views might be the evidence is overwhelming that these differences are principally due to social factors (Sanders 1934).

Why is it that these racial ideologists refuse to acknowledge, even to consider, that social factors may be the principal causes responsible for the differences in learning abilities of different "racial" groups? Learning ability is highly correlated with social class within the same ethnic group (Davidson 1943; Hunt 1969; Lesser, Fifer, and Clark 1965). What racists fail to understand is that in man "race" is, for all practical purposes, a social concept and an institutionalized way of behavior, a special form of social class, a caste status, and that as such it is subject to all the influences and consequences that flow from such facts.

That a significant genetic element contributes to the basic intelligence potential of every individual is beyond dispute. It should, however, be clear that, like every other genetic potential, the development of intelligence is perhaps more than any other trait dependent on the kind of environmental stimulations to which it is exposed. Instead of dismissing such environmental factors as unimportant in order to sustain even the veriest semblance of his claims, Jensen should have carefully investigated the possible effects of such environmental factors upon IQ test results. This he conspicuously failed to do, and for this reason alone his claims would have to be wholly rejected. To assign, as he does, a good eighty percent of an individual's intelligence to genetic factors and a mere twenty percent to environmental influences constitutes not only a scientifically groundless assumption but also a wholly indefensible one. For there exists a vast body of scientific evidence which indicates not that genetic potentials or environmental ones are more important than the other, but that both are of the greatest importance for the adequate development of intelligence. I have already made reference to some of the evidence indicating the damage that malnutrition can do to genetic potentials for intelligence. The evidence indicating the damage capable of being done by unfavorable socio-economic conditions to the development of intelligence is even more extensive and conclusive. This evidence is set out in hundreds of independent studies ranging from Gladys Schwesinger's 1933 volume *Heredity and Environment* to the most recent publication on the subject, namely Cancro's symposium on *Intelligence: Genetic and Environmental Influences* (1971), Birch and Gussow's book on *Disadvantaged Children* (1969), and Hurley's book on *Poverty and Mental Retardation* (1969), not to mention many others.

The universal conclusion to which these researches point is that no matter what the quality of the genetic potentials for intelligence may be in any individual, the expression of those potentials will be significantly influenced by his total environment. Poverty as such is not necessarily either a necessary or a sufficient condition in the production of intellectual deficits, for if nutrition and the home cultural environment are adequate, the child will suffer no handicapping effects. But if nutrition is poor, health care deficient, housing debasing, family income low, family disorganization prevalent, discipline anarchic, ghettoization more or less complete, personal worth consistently diminished, expectations low, and aspirations frustrated, as well as numerous other environmental handicaps, then one may expect the kind of failures in intellectual development that are so often gratuitously attributed to genetic factors. Those who make such attributions fail to understand how dependent the development of intelligence is upon the reduction of such conditions of privation, frustration, and hopelessness (Watson 1970). When the effects of such postnatal environmental factors are combined with the adverse effects of prenatal ones, there emerges a continuum of psycho-social, as well as psycho-physical casualty, which renders it utterly nonsensical to compare casualties of such environments with the products of average middle class environments by whom and on whom IQ tests were devised. It is not simply the culture of poverty or even the poverty of culture or any other one single factor, but the combination of many socio-environmental factors, which produces the sociogenic deficits so irresponsibly attributed to genetic factors. As Gladys Schwesinger pointed out at the conclusion of her book *Heredity and Environment* in 1933, "the problem of heredity and environment is not a general problem, but is specific to each individual, to each of his characteristics, and to each environment" (1933:465). In the development of so complex an ability as intelligence, making every allowance for possible differences in genetic endowment, the environment is of paramount importance. Just as the individual learns to speak, with vocabulary, imagery, and accent according to environmental influences that have been operative upon him, so he learns, within the limits of his genetic capacities, the vocabulary, imagery, and accent of intelligence, according to the environmental influences with which he has interacted. As Bodmer and Cavalli-Sforza have put it, "any given test . . . depends on the ability acquired at a given age, which is inevitably the result of the combination of innate ability and the experience of the subject. Intelligence tests are therefore at most tests of achieved ability" (1970:19) . And that is precisely the point. If seriously handicapping impediments are placed in the way of the individual's development of any capacity he will to that extent simply fail to achieve that ability, for abilities are trained capacities. Limiting environments place limits upon the development of abilities. In the matter of problem-solving, that is to say, intelligence, Harlow found that rhesus monkeys subjected to ambiguous rewards for tasks performed, so that no specific perceptual clues were available to the animals, were not nearly as effective problem-solvers as those in the control group who were consistently rewarded. Harlow thus showed that the learning sets which make insight possible do not come ready-made, but must be acquired, and that once acquired they increase the capacity of the organism to solve certain problems (Harlow 1949, 1958). Thompson and Heron have shown that pet-reared dogs in a variety of situations behave more intelligently than their litter-mates who have been caged for the first eight months of their lives (Thompson and Heron 1954). All animals thus far studied show the effects of early experience or its deprivation in much the same ways (Bronfenbrenner 1968).

Bennett, Rosenzweig, and Diamond have shown that exposure of rats to different environments—enriched, colony, or impoverished —leads to characteristic changes in wet and dry weight of samples of rat brain, in enzymatic activity, and in depth of cerebral cortex. Impoverished animals were caged singly, colony animals two or three per cage, and enriched animals ten or twelve per larger cage includ-ing toys. In every case, dry weight depth of cerebral cortex, enzy-matic activity, and problem solving behavior, were increased by ex-posure to enriched environment as compared with standard colony and impoverished conditions (Bennett, Rosenzweig, and Diamond 1969; Rosenzweig, Krech, Bennett, and Diamond 1968). In mice, Henderson found that an enriched environment resulted in an in-crease in brain weight (1970).

Since the internal consistency of the evidence for other animals fully agrees with that obtained in studies of man, there can remain little doubt that for the development of innumerable behavioral traits, but especially for the development of intelligence the stimula-tion of certain kinds of social experience is indispensably necessary (Light and Smith 1969; Stinchcombe 1969). It is, in a word, experi-ences of an encouraging kind, as contrasted to experiences of a dis-couraging kind, the experiences of an advantaging kind that count, as contrasted with experiences of a disadvantaging kind.

When we consider the complexity of the factors operating upon the child the sociogenic brain damage done in man must be very considerable indeed, for there can be no question that brain dam-age is involved when size, weight, failure of cortical development, quantity and size of brain cells, and enzymatic activity of the brain are the effects of a socially impoverished environment.

Jensen so completely fails to understand the nature of socially dis-advantaging conditions he actually believes that the children of Blacks and Whites of similar income level enjoy equal cultural and other environmental advantages. Hence, since these children, ac-cording to Jensen, enjoy similar environmental experiences, the differences in IQ test results must be due to genetic factors. What Jensen fails to understand is that income level alone does not determine the quality of cultural background, and that it is quite unsound to equate the two. There is no income level at which Blacks enjoy the same basic opportunities as Whites. By basic opportunities I mean a sustaining cultural background of stimulation which encourages the growth and development of aspirations for achievement, a cultural background in which one does not suffer from malnutrition of the body or the mind, in which one has not suffered severe emotional, economic, social, and educational privations, but to which, in most of these respects, a positive rather than a negative sign is attached.

The truth is that at no time have Blacks of any income group enjoyed anything approaching equal basic opportunities with Whites (Montagu 1970). It is, therefore, quite unsound to attribute to genetic factors what may well be due to environmental ones (Klineberg 1954).

What is quite certain is that IQ's vary with environmental experience. It is, for example, well known that American Indians generally test out at about eighty IQ points. But, interestingly enough, when oil is discovered on Indian land and the Indians are permitted to share in the accruing profits, there is a spectacular rise in Indian IQ's. There is nothing mysterious about this. The oil simply facilitates the lubrication of intelligence potentials by making the conditions available which enable Indian children to enjoy a social and economic environment similar to that enjoyed by White children. Under such conditions, among the Osage Indians of Oklahoma, for example, Rohrer found that on one test, the Goodenough "Draw-a-man" test, the White children obtained an average IQ of 103, and the Indian children an average of 104. On a second test, using language, the Indian children scored 100 and the White children scored 98 (Rohrer 1942).

Similarly, Garth found that a group of Indian children living in White foster homes obtained an average IQ of 102, which is a quite significant improvement over an IQ of 80. The brothers and sisters of this group still living on the Reservation obtained an average IQ of 87.5 (Garth 1935). [See chaps. 7 and 8 of this volume.—Ed.]

Clearly, the environmental differences were principally responsible for the differences in the scores of these children. There is no question of brain damage being involved here—simply a difference in environment. Nor, for that matter was a difference in genetic intelligence involved, for clearly that is not what these test results reflected; what they reflected was a difference in environmental experience acting upon genetic potentials for the ability to respond to IQ tests. It is not that the lower testing siblings were any less intelligent than their higher testing siblings, but that they were less experienced in the requirements necessary to meet the challenges of those tests.

Since genetic factors are involved in virtually all forms of behavior, there can be little doubt that such factors play a significant role in performance on IQ tests. But that is a very different thing from claiming that IQ tests measure the genetic contribution to intelligence. Scarr-Salapatek has published a study in which she found differences in heritability of IQ scores in Black and White and in social and class groups (1971). The differences are in the expected directions and could have been predicted. Scarr-Salapatek sees the variance in performance as difference, *not* as deficit, and she welcomes these differences as contributing to the greater enrichment and variety of humanity. "To the extent," she writes "that better, more supportive environments can be provided for all children, genetic variance and mean scores will increase for all groups" (1971: 1295). Indeed, "equality of opportunity" will lead "to bigger and better genotype-phenotype correlations" (1971:1295), but meanwhile, it needs to be emphasized, so long as the inequalities in opportunities remain, so long will the misery and poor performance on IQ tests and in life situations remain for millions of the socially deprived.

There are many flaws in IQ tests, and among those usually overlooked by those who administer and evaluate these tests is the fact that a difference of as much as twenty points can be produced in IQ scores depending upon the mood or attitude of the testee. Feelings toward the person administering the test can be an important factor in influencing performance on tests. Katz, Heuchy, and Allen (1968) found that Negro boys of grade-school age performed better on verbal learning tasks with Negro examiners than with White examiners. Watson found that West Indian students in a London secondary school in a working class neighborhood scored an average of ten points less on IQ tests than when the same tests were falsely described as an experiment to help curriculum. Watson, who is White, also found that when the tests were given by his assistant, a "very black" West Indian, the scores typically climbed (Watson 1970).

Similarly, Katz has found that Black students did better on IQ tests when they were deceived into believing that their intelligence was not being tested. Black students, when they were freed of anxiety about intellectual performance, achieved higher IQ scores under a White investigator than a Black one (Deutsch, Katz, and Jensen 1968).

With little expectation of overcoming the judgment of their intellectual inferiority, which they knew to be held by many White Americans, the students' motivation was low, and so were their scores. But when the IQ test was disguised as something else, human ambition soared. As long as their intelligence was not being evaluated, they felt more challenged to show the White examiner what they could do than one of their own kind.

The expectation of inadequate performance on IQ tests undoubtedly contributes to the lower performance of Blacks on these tests. Conversely, confidence bolstered by some successes raises scores by five to ten points.

I am not aware that either Jensen or Scarr-Salapatek made any allowance for such factors.

Cooper and Zubek in an interesting experiment have shown how in different genetic lines different environments may serve either to develop or depress problem-solving capacities. These investigators used two lines of rats whose ability to find their way through a maze had been especially selected by selective breeding. When rats from the "bright" and "dull" lines were raised for a whole generation in a restricted environment which differed from the normal laboratory environment, no differences between the lines could be found. The bright and dull performed at the same level. When both were raised in the same stimulating environment, both did almost equally well. In a normal environment, bright rats made 120 errors, whereas the dull ones made 168. In a restricted environment, both made about 170 errors, but in a stimulating environment, the bright made 112 errors while the dull made 120 (Cooper and Zubek 1958).

Levitsky and Barnes (1972) found that early malnutrition and isolation in rats during the first seven weeks of postnatal life led to various behavioral sequelae. Compared with the controls the experimental animals showed a significant increase in open field locomotion, an increase, but not statistically significant, in mutual grooming, a reduction in following response, an increase in fighting time, and a marked depression in exploratory behavior. These investigators found that in all the observed responses, except fighting, whatever effect early malnutrition produced, it was always exaggerated by environmental isolation and depressed by environmental stimulation. They found, also, that the behavioral effects of the malnutrition were completely eliminated in most cases by additional stimulation early in life.

The theoretical mechanisms the authors suggest as possibly explaining the mechanisms through which malnutrition and environmental stimulation may interact to produce long term behavioral changes are two. This explanation applies with equal cogency to the social deprivation syndrome.

Malnutrition may alter the experience or perception of the environment during early development by rendering the organism physiologically less capable of receiving and/or integrating environmental information. Decreases in brain size, brain DNA, myelinization, cortical dendritic growth, brain cholinesterase content, and brain norepinephrine control have all been reported in malnourished animals. Environmental stimulation produces changes in brain norepinephrine, cholinesterase, as well as cortical dendritic growth. Hence, malnutrition during a critical period of development may produce the changes which render inoperative the physiological mechanisms that are responsible for the long term effects of early stimulation.

Another mechanism through which early malnutrition and environmental variables may interact may be purely behavioral in nature. Malnutrition may produce behavior that is incompatible with the incorporation of environmental information necessary for optimum cognitive growth. In the case of a malnourished animal, the behavior may be primarily food oriented and in the case of a malnourished child, the behavior may be expressed as apathy and social withdrawal (Latham 1968).

Thus, specific kinds of information or specific behavioral responses which may be required for optimum cognitive development as reflected by test behavior or educational performance may be absent or depressed in the malnourished child as a result of a higher priority of responses elicited by the malnutrition.

The demonstration of a behavioral interaction between early nutritional conditions and the environment of young animals not only demonstrates the complexity of understanding determinants of behavior, but also points out the profundity of early experience and early nutrition as major contributors to ultimate adult behavior (Levitsky and Barnes 1972:70–71).

The power of the environment is clearly very considerable indeed, and the earlier it affects the developing organism the more substantive are its effects. The point I wish to make here is that brain damage is no less brain damage when the social stimuli necessary for mental development are inadequate or rendered ambiguous or confusing, than when the physical nutrition necessary for adequate cerebral development is insufficient. The brain damage done by social deprivation, even though it may be more occult, is, in its behavioral consequences, at least as substantial as that done by physical malnutrition.

To conclude, the evidence clearly indicates that during the first three years, when the basic foundations and organization of the brain are in process of construction, inadequate provision and poor quality of experience may seriously affect the fabric of the brain, of which the mind is presumably a function. In such cases, the brain and mind are rendered incapable of later organization at levels of cognitive integration matching those achieved by others who have not suffered such sociogenic damage.

In such cases, the brain may not have been damaged in quite the same manner as it may be by physical malnutrition, but the damage done by social malnutrition is nonetheless real. This, we may postulate, consists in the disabling failure of organization which, both structurally and functionally, renders it extremely difficult if not impossible for individuals to respond appropriately to many of the challenges of the environment with the competence that their genetic potentials would, under the organizing stimulation of an adequate social environment, have permitted. Social malnourishment, both structurally and functionally, can be just as brain/mind damaging as physical malnourishment. Such sociogenic malnourishment affects the brains of millions of human beings not only in the United States but all over the world. It is a form of brain damage which has received far too little attention. Yet it constitutes an epidemic problem of major proportions. What it calls for is, first, the recognition that the problem exists, second that it can only be solved by those improvements in the environment which will assure every newborn baby the realization of his birthright, which is development of his potentialities to the optimum.

We are each of us part of the problem. The question is whether we are going to remain parts of the problem or make ourselves part of the solution.

References

AMBROSE, A., ED. 1969. *Stimulation in Early Infancy.* New York: Academic Press.

BASS, N. H., M. G. NETSKY, AND E. YOUNG. 1970a. Effect of Neonatal Malnutrition on Developing Cerebrum. *Archives of Neurology* 23:289–302.

——. 1970b. Microchemical and Histologic Study of Myelin Formation in the Rat. *Archives of Neurology* 23:303–313.

BENNETT, E. L., M. R. ROSENZWEIG, AND M. C. DIAMOND. 1969. Rat Brain: Effects of Environmental Enrichment on Wet and Dry Weights. *Science* 163:825–826.

BIRCH, H. G., ED. 1964. *Brain Damage in Children: Its Biological and Social Aspects.* Baltimore: Williams & Wilkins.

BIRCH, H. G., AND J. D. GUSSOW. 1969. *Disadvantaged Children.* New York: Harcourt, Brace & World.

BODMER, W. F., AND L. L. CAVALLI-SFORZA. 1970. Intelligence and Race. *Scientific American* 223:19–29.

BRONFENBRENNER, U. 1968. Early Deprivation in Mammals: A Cross-Species Analysis. In *Early Experience and Behavior.* G. Newton and S. Levene, eds. Springfield, Illinois: C C Thomas. Pp. 627–764.

CANCRO, R., ED. 1971. *Intelligence: Genetic and Environmental.* New York: Grune & Stratton.

COGHILL, G. E. 1929. *Anatomy and the Problem of Behaviour.* Cambridge: At the University Press.

COOPER, R. M., AND J. P. ZUBEK. 1958. Effects of Enriched and Restricted Early Environments on the Learning Ability of Bright and Dull Rats. *Canadian Journal of Psychology* 12:159–164.

CRAVIOTO, J. 1970. Complexity of Factors Involved in Protein-Calorie Malnutrition. In *Malnutrition Is a Problem of Ecology*. P. György and O. L. Kline, eds. Basel and New York: Karger. Pp. 7–22.

DAVIDSON, H. H. 1943. *Personality and Economic Background*. New York: King's Crown Press.

DAVISON, A. N., AND J. DOBBING. 1968. Myelination as a Vulnerable Period in Brain Development. *British Medical Bulletin* 22:40–44.

DEUTSCH, M., AND ASSOCIATES. 1967. *The Disadvantaged Child*. New York: Basic Books.

DEUTSCH, M., I. KATZ, AND R. JENSEN, EDS. 1968. *Social Class, Race, and Psychological Development*. New York: Holt, Rinehart & Winston.

DOBBING, J. 1964. The Influence of Nutrition on the Development of the Brain. Proceedings of the Royal Society, London, Series B. Biological Sciences 159:503–509.

––––––. 1968. Effects of Experimental Undernutrition on Development of the Nervous System. In *Malnutrition, Learning and Behavior*. N. S. Scrimshaw and J. E. Gordon, eds. Cambridge: M.I.T. Press. Pp. 181–202.

––––––. 1970a. Undernutrition and the Developing Brain. *American Journal of Diseases of Childhood* 120:411–415.

––––––. 1970b. Food for Thinking. *New Scientist* 46:636–637.

DRILLIEN, C. M., AND E. M. WILKINSON. 1964. Emotional Stress and Mongoloid Births. *Developmental Medicine and Child Neurology* 6:140–143.

EDSON, L. 1969. The Theory That I.Q. Is Largely Determined by the Genes. *New York Times Magazine*, August 31. Pp. 10–11, 40–41, 43–47.

EELLS, K., AND OTHERS. 1951. *Intelligence and Cultural Differences*. Chicago: University of Chicago Press.

EICHENWALD, H. F., AND P. C. FRY. 1969. Nutrition and Learning. *Science* 163:644–648.

GANTT, W. HORSLEY. 1950. Disturbances in Sexual Function During Periods of Stress. In *Life Stress and Bodily Disease*. H. G. Wolff, S. G. Wolff, Jr., and C. C. Hare, eds. Baltimore: Williams & Wilkins. Pp. 1030–1050.

GARTH, T. R. 1935. A Study of the Foster Indian Child in the White Home. *Psychological Bulletin* 32:708–709.

GÖLLNITZ, G. 1963–64. Über die Problematik der Neurosen im Kindesalter. *Ideggyogyaszatio Szemle* 16:97–108.

GROTBERG, E., ED. 1969. *Critical Issues in Research Related to Disadvantaged Children*. Princeton, New Jersey: Educational Testing Service.

GYÖRGY, P., AND O. L. KLINE, EDS. 1970. *Malnutrition Is a Problem of Ecology*. Basel and New York: Karger.

HARLOW, H. F. 1949. The Formation of Learning Sets. *Psychological Review* 56:51–65.

———. 1958. Learning and Satiation of Response in Intrinsically Motivated Complex Puzzle Performance by Monkeys. *Journal of Comparative and Physiological Psychology* 43:289–294.

HENDERSON, N. D. 1970. Brain Weight Increases Resulting from Environmental Enrichment: A Directional Dominance in Mice. *Science* 169:776–778.

HUNT, J. McV. 1961. *Intelligence and Experience*. New York: Ronald Press Co.

———. 1969. *The Challenge of Incompetence and Poverty*. Urbana: University of Illinois Press.

HURLEY, R. L. 1969. *Poverty and Mental Retardation: A Causal Relationship*. New York: Random House.

IAGRASHI, M., K. TOHMA, AND M. OZAMA. 1965. Pathogenesis of Psychogenic Amenorrhea and Anovulation. *International Journal of Fertility* 10:311–319.

JENSEN, A. 1969. How Much Can We Boost I.Q. and Scholastic Achievement? *Harvard Educational Review* 39:1–123.

JOFFE, J. M. 1969. *Prenatal Determinants of Behaviour*. New York: Pergamon Press.

KASE, N. G. 1969. The Ovary. In *Duncan's Diseases of Metabolism*. Vol. 2. P. K. Bondy, ed. Philadelphia: Saunders. Pp. 1191–1226.

KATZ, I., T. HEUCHY, AND H. ALLEN. 1968. Effects of Race of Tester, Approval, Disapproval, and Need on Negro Children's Learning. *Journal of Personality and Social Research* 8:38–42.

KLINEBERG, O. 1954. *Social Psychology*. Revised edition. New York: Holt, Rinehart & Winston.

LATHAM, M. C. 1968. In *Calorie and Protein Deficiencies*. R. A. McCance and E. M. Widdowson, eds. New York and London: Cambridge University Press. Pp. 23–32.

LESSER, G. S., G. FIFER, AND D. H. CLARK. 1965. Mental Abilities of Children from Different Social-Class and Cultural Groups. Monographs of the Society for Research in Child Growth and Development 30(4).

LEVITAN, M., AND A. MONTAGU. 1971. *A Textbook of Human Genetics*. New York: Oxford University Press.

LEVITSKY, D. A., AND R. H. BARNES. 1972. Nutritional and Environmental Interactions in the Behavioral Development of the Rat: Long Term Behavioral Effects. *Science* 176:68–71.

LIGHT, R. J., AND P. V. SMITH. 1969. Social Allocation Models of Intelligence. *Harvard Educational Review* 39:484–510.

MAY, J. M., AND H. LEMONS. 1969. The Ecology of Malnutrition. *Journal of the American Medical Association* 207:2401–2405.

MICHAEL, R. P., ED. 1968. *Endocrinology and Human Behavior.* New York: Oxford University Press.

MÖNCKEBERG, F. 1968. Mental Retardation from Malnutrition: 'Irreversible . . .' *Journal of the American Medical Association* 206:30–31.

———. 1970. Factors Conditioning Malnutrition in Latin America, With Special Reference to Chile. Advice for a Volunteer Action. In *Malnutrition Is a Problem of Ecology.* P. György and O. L. Kline, eds. Basel and New York: Karger. Pp. 23–33.

MONTAGU, A. 1961. Neonatal and Infant Immaturity in Man. *Journal of the American Medical Association* 178:56–57.

———. 1962. *Prenatal Influences.* Springfield, Illinois: C C Thomas.

———. 1974. *Man's Most Dangerous Myth: The Fallacy of Race.* Fifth edition. New York: Oxford University Press.

———. 1970. Just What Is "Equal Opportunity"? *Vista* 6:23–25, 56.

OSLER, S. F., AND R. E. COOKE, EDS. 1965. *The Biosocial Basis of Mental Retardation.* Baltimore: The Johns Hopkins Press.

REISSMAN, F. 1962. *The Culturally Deprived Child.* New York: Harper & Row.

ROHRER, J. H. 1942. The Test Intelligence of Osage Indians. *Journal of Social Psychology* 16:99–105.

ROSENZWEIG, M. R., D. KRECH, E. L. BENNETT, AND M. C. DIAMOND. 1968. Modifying Brain Chemistry and Anatomy by Enrichment or Impoverishment of Experience. In *Early Experience and Behavior.* G. Newton and S. Levine, eds. Springfield, Illinois: C C Thomas. Pp. 258–298.

SANDERS, B. S. 1934. *Environment and Growth.* Baltimore: Warwick & York.

SCARR-SALAPATEK, S. 1971. Race, Social Class, and IQ. *Science* 174:1285–1295.

SCHAPIRO, S., AND K. R. VUKOVICH. 1970. Early Experience Effects upon Cortical Dendrites: A Proposed Model for Development. *Science* 165:293–294.

SCHILDKRAUT, J. J., AND S. S. KETY. 1967. Biogenic Amines and Emotion. *Science* 156:21–30.

SCHWESINGER, G. 1933. *Heredity and Environment.* New York: Macmillan.

SELYE, H. 1950. *Stress.* Montreal: Acta, Inc.

STERMAN, M. B., D. J. McGINTY, AND A. M. ADINOLFI, EDS. 1971. *Brain Development and Behavior.* New York: Academic Press.

STIEVE, H. 1942. Der Einfluss von Angst und Psychischer Eregnung auf Bau und Funktion der Weiblichen Geschlechtsorgane. *Zintralblatt für Gynäkologie* 66:1698–1708.

————. 1949. Anatomisch nachweisbare Vorgänge im Eierstock des Menschen und ihre Umweltbedingte Steuerung. *Geburtshiffe und Frauenheilkunde* 9:639:644.

————. 1951. *Der Einfluss des Nervens Systems auf Bau und Totigkeit der Geschlechtsorgane des Menschen.* Stuttgart: Georg Thieme.

STINCHCOMBE, A. L. 1969. Environment: The Cumulation of Events. *Harvard Educational Review* 39:511–522.

STOTT, D. H. 1961. Mongolism Related to Emotional Shock in Early Pregnancy. *Vita Humana* 4:57–76.

————. 1966. *Troublesome Children.* New York: Humanities Press.

SWANSON, C. P. 1964. *The Cell.* Second Edition. Englewood Cliffs, New Jersey: Prentice-Hall.

TAYLOR, H. C. 1950. Life Situations, Emotions and Gynecologic Pain Associated with Congestion. In *Life Stress and Bodily Disease.* H. G. Wolff, S. G. Wolff, Jr., and C. C. Hare, eds. Baltimore: Williams & Wilkins. Pp. 1051–1056.

THOMPSON, W. R., AND W. HERON. 1954. The Effects of Restricting Early Experience on the Problem-Solving Capacity of Dogs. *Canadian Journal of Psychology* 8:17–31.

TOBACH, E., L. R. ARONSON, AND E. SHAW, EDS. 1971. *The Biopsychology of Development.* New York: Academic Press.

WATSON, P. 1970. How Race Affects I.Q. *New Society* (London), July 16: pp. 103–104.

WINICK, M. 1968. Nutrition and Cell Growth. *Nutrition Reviews* 26:195–197.

————. 1970. Fetal Malnutrition and Growth Processes. *Hospital Practice,* May: 33–41.

WINICK, M., AND P. ROSSO. 1969a. The Effect of Severe Malnutrition on Cellular Growth of the Human Brain. *Pediatric Research* 3:181–184.

————. 1969b. Head Circumference and Cellular Growth of the Brain in Normal and Marasmic Children. *Journal of Pediatrics* 74:774–778.

WOLFF, H. G. 1968. *Stress and Disease.* Second Edition. Springfield, Illinois: C C Thomas.

ZAMENHOF, S., E. VAN MARTHENS, AND F. L. MARGOLIS. 1968. DNA (Cell Number) and Protein Deficiency in Neonatal Brain: Alteration by Maternal Dietary Protein Restriction. *Science* 160:322–323.

————. 1971. DNA (Cell Number) in Neonatal Brain: Second Generation (F_2) Alteration by Maternal (F_0) Dietary Protein Restriction. *Science* 172:850–851.

6   In the last selection, it was suggested that a social environment which failed to stimulate a child adequately in the first few years so important to the growth of his nervous system, can seriously affect the quality of functioning of his brain. This, in turn, leads to deficits in learning and performance on IQ tests and other achievement tests that assume exposure to certain kinds of experiences. The discussion related chiefly to children of minority cultures, of low socioeconomic status, whose failures in achievement are much too readily blamed on their "racial" identity without regard to the conditions within which they develop. The selection that follows illustrates that even in an environment that is socioeconomically privileged, conditions may exist that so seriously affect the growth and development of children that they appear to be retarded as if from constitutional causes.

The report, "Environmental Retardation (Hospitalism) in Infants Living in Families," * by Drs. Rose W. Coleman and Sally Provence, discusses the cases of two children, a boy of seventeen months and a girl of three years. We learn from this discussion that infants reared in their own families, and in families of good socioeconomic status, may suffer severe functional mental retardation if they are exposed to a cold emotional climate. As we shall see from the contributions which follow this one, the emotional climate doesn't necessarily have to be cold to produce severe developmental retardation. Inadequacies in the parents, and especially in the mother, during the early months and years of the child's development may produce a climate—now hot, now cold, now confused—leading to a final resigned acceptance of the hopelessness of the situation which can be equally if not more damaging than the simple inadequacy of the ability to love (Note 1).

There are undoubtedly thousands of middle- and upper-class homes in which the emotionally refrigerated atmosphere results in the more or less severe crippling of the children raised

* From *Pediatrics*, vol. 19 (1957), pp. 285–92. Reprinted by permission of Sally Provence and the American Academy of Pediatrics.

At the time this paper was written Drs. Coleman and Provence were affiliated with the Department of Pediatrics, School of Medicine and Child Study Center, Yale University and Grace-New Haven Community Hospital, New Haven, Conn.

Appreciation is expressed to Dr. Ernst Kris, Dr. Milton J. E. Senn and Dr. Morris Green for suggestions and comments which have been valuable in the preparation of this paper.

in them. This may vary from severe retardation to the appearance of normality, but the normality is only superficial; the emotional damage is deep and often permanent (Note 2).

NOTE 1: Ashley Montagu, *The Direction of Human Development,* revised edition (New York: Hawthorn Books, 1970). John Bowlby, *Attachment and Loss,* 2 vols. (New York: Basic Books, 1969, 1973). NOTE 2: See, for example, Swanberg's biography of William Randolph Hearst and Orson Welles' film *Citizen Kane.* See also Errol Flynn, *My Wicked, Wicked Ways* (New York: Putnam's, 1959). This subject is also discussed in the chapter "To Grow or Not to Grow" in the volume *Growing With Children* of the series *Human Development Books)* of which the present volume is a part.

ENVIRONMENTAL RETARDATION (HOSPITALISM) IN INFANTS LIVING IN FAMILIES

Rose W. Coleman, M.D.,
and Sally Provence, M.D.

The syndrome of retarded development in infancy due to insufficient physical, social and emotional stimulation from another person has been described by various authors. It has been called environmental retardation by Gesell and Amatruda,[1] hospitalism by Spitz,[2] affect deprivation by Lowrey,[3] and emotional deprivation by Bakwin.[4] Published reports have appeared primarily in the psychologic and psychiatric literature, although Bakwin[4,5] has drawn attention to the syndrome in the pediatric literature. The literature and case reports almost exclusively describe its occurrence in institutionalized infants. Gesell and Amatruda[1] suggest that it can occur in children living in families but give no clinical data. The presence of the syndrome in family infants requires emphasis and wider recognition. It should be carefully considered in the differential diagnosis

---

[1] [Superscript numerals throughout this chapter refer to items in References, pp. 87 and 88.—Ed.]

of developmental retardation in infancy, since prognosis is good if proper treatment is instituted.

In this paper we present two patients who developed the clinical syndrome of environmental retardation in a family setting. The etiology, insufficient stimulation from the mother, is in both cases similar to the etiology of environmental retardation in the institutionalized infant. The resulting clinical picture is also strikingly similar.

CASE REPORTS

Case 1

B, a 17-month-old white boy, was admitted to the pediatric ward with a presumptive diagnosis of mental retardation. The referring pediatrician, who had cared for the child from the age of 13 months, had become increasingly concerned about the delay in his motor development, small size, the unexplained elevation of the leukocyte count and a feeding problem. The following data were obtained from the mother in a series of three interviews.

Family history. B was the first-born child of parents who were college graduates. The father was an industrial designer and the mother had been a successful elementary school teacher prior to her pregnancy. She expressed enjoyment of school age children. Pregnancy, labor and delivery were normal. A male sibling, born when B was 13 months old had colic for the first 3 months of life and was described as a poor feeder. Nonetheless, the mother found him easier to care for and more vigorous and outgoing than the patient.

Feeding. The mother's greatest concern at the time of hospitalization was the feeding problem which had had its onset at birth. Birth weight of the patient was 2863 gm and he was a full-term, normal, healthy infant. Formula feedings were given from the beginning. He sucked efficiently but fed slowly and fell asleep during feedings. She thumped his feet to keep him awake, was concerned if he did not drain his bottle, and annoyed at having to spend 45 to 60 minutes for each feeding. There was never any vomiting, spitting out of food, diarrhea or colic. He received a multivitamin supplement regularly from the early weeks of life. Solids were begun at 3 months and at first were more easily given than the bottle; later the mother could feed solids only by distracting him. Forced feeding and insistence alternated with attempts at persuasion or removal of the food in anger. Feeding became situations around which the mother and B actively struggled. The mother recalled no period of his life when she considered the feeding satisfactory or pleasant and at times had found it painfully intolerable. The atmosphere during feeding was charged with feelings of anger or anxiety or was characterized by depression in which she felt disgusted, defeated or indifferent. There were few opportunities for B to have the experience of being fed by a person who could enjoy it, feel comfortable about it, and help him develop positive attitudes toward eating. For 3 to 4 months prior to admission he oftentimes pushed away the feeding hand and had been throwing food or the spoon when attempts were made to encourage self-feeding.

Development. The mother described B as being an infant who from birth cried very little and was content to spend the greater part of each day in his crib in his room alone while she worked in another part of the house. She could recall no pleasure in caring for him as a young infant. He smiled at 3 months of age. When he was 4 months old she became pregnant for the second time. At 7 months, as B was beginning to sit alone, the mother's father committed suicide. His death was a great shock to her and there followed a prolonged period of grief and depression from which she found it difficult to arouse herself sufficiently to take care of B. When he was about 11 months old (the sixth or seventh month of her pregnancy) she shifted some of his care to his father since she felt both the need of help and the need to accustom B to a plan which they could continue after the birth of the new baby. She described her husband as willing to help but finding little enjoyment in the feeding, putting to bed, etc., preferring to spend his time working around the house rather than with B. The maternal grandmother and paternal grandparents saw B about once a week and from the mother's descriptions one must conclude that these were his warmest and most spontaneous contacts with people. At 1 year of age he had three words which he stopped using following the birth of his sibling. He crept at 14 months, pulled to stand at 16 months and at 17 months cruised and walked with two hands held. The mother felt that his development began to improve at around 13 months and was relatively better at the time of admission than it had been earlier. This improvement consisted of more interest in locomotion, more interest in toys and more ability to designate clearly what he did and did not want. By the time of admission he waved good-by, played pat-a-cake, identified his eyes and nose by pointing and had a vocabulary of four to six words.

Physical findings. On admission B was a small undernourished infant. Head circumference was 46 cm (third to tenth percentile). Anterior fontanel measured 3 cm by 5 cm. Weight was 7.8 kg (below the third percentile). Height was not recorded. Serial heights through the eight month of life reported by the referring physician had been consistently around the fiftieth percentile. There was scanty subcutaneous fat, and muscle tone was generally poor. He had a small pilonidal sinus. Remainder of physical examination, including neurologic and ophthalmoscopic appraisal, was normal.

At first, B was often irritable in the presence of staff members, and apathetic, sad or depressed when left alone. He reacted to the appearance of any new person by crying or by looking apprehensive. This discomfort could be overcome by giving him time to make an adjustment. He was invariably upset for a few minutes by a change from one situation to another; e.g., if he were moved from crib to high chair, from chair to floor, or picked up or put down. Once the transition was made, he was again comfortable. He had some interest in play materials which he used partly for his own amusement and partly in a game with the adult in which he threw the offered toys to the floor in a provocative, teasing way. He enjoyed being held and talked to and made some attempts to initiate social contact by smiling, vocalizing or offering a toy, after he had familiarized himself with a particular adult.

Laboratory findings. Chemical determinations of nonprotein nitrogen, total protein with albumin and globulin, glucose, CO_2, chloride, sodium, potassium, cholesterol, and butyl extractable iodine in the blood gave normal results. Stool examinations were negative. Nose and throat cultures were normal. Urinalyses were normal except for occasional traces of reducing substance which was not considered significant in view of the normal fasting blood sugar. Ferric chloride test for phenylpyruvic acid in the urine was negative.

Erythrocyte counts were 5,500,000/mm³ and 5,300,000 mm³ on two occasions with hemoglobin concentrations of 11.5 and 12.9 gm/100 ml. The mean corpuscular volume, the mean corpuscular hemoglobin and the mean corpuscular hemoglobin concentration were normal. Sedimentation rate was normal. Leukocytes were 24,350/mm³ with a normal differential count. Two subsequent leukocyte counts were 14,500/mm³ and 15,475/mm³, both with normal differential counts. No disease process was disclosed which would account for the leukocytosis. Electroencephalogram, roentgenograms and chest, skull and long bones for bone age were normal.

Gesell developmental examination. On the day after admission his gross motor development, at the 48-week level (6 months below age), was the area of greatest retardation. He walked with two hands held and cruised about the crib and playpen. Fine motor development, including grasping patterns, ability to manipulate, and hand-eye co-ordination were adequate for his age. In the adaptive sphere he had two successes at or above his chronological age, and some failures at his age level. Language consisted of a reported four to six words and no jargon. He showed some interest in the picture book and in it identified the specific familiar object (the dog). His response to people consisted of initial fearfulness followed by tentative attempts to initiate social contact, and by provocative casting of objects offered, with obvious intent to elicit some kind of a response from the adult. The diagnostic impression from the developmental examination was that this was an emotionally deprived and insufficiently stimulated child rather than a mentally retarded child.

Course. A 3-week therapeutic trial was offered in the hospital setting to alleviate the feeding problem and provide social, emotional and physical stimulation. Ideally, the way of providing this therapy would have been to make one interested and constant mother substitute responsible for his total care. In the ward setting the ideal arrangement was impossible, but it was approximated by limiting the number of mother substitutes to two interested nurses one or the other of whom was responsible for all of his care during his waking hours. Under the influence of these two responsive, warm adults who fed, played and talked with him, and encouraged him to move about, he made significant improvement. They helped him with feeding but did not force and they permitted him to get his hands in the food and to feed himself as he was ready to do so. At first there was much messiness and throwing both of food and the spoon and he lost 300 gm in weight. After the first week he gave up the throwing behavior and some of the messiness and became actively interested in self-feeding with the friendly adult at hand to assist as he asked for it. He became strikingly less apathetic, used more language, smiled and laughed more. His interest in toys became more sustained and constructive. He moved about much more freely and with greater vigor and enjoyment. Weight on discharge was 420 gm above admission weight. In the 3 months prior to admission there had been no weight gain.

Developmental evaluation at the end of the 3-week period revealed he had gained 8 weeks in gross motor development, 2 months in adaptive, 3 months in language and 2 months in social development.

Efforts to help the mother with modification of her feeding methods through inviting her to be present at B's feeding time and receiving help from the nurse were unsuccessful as the family lived out of town and could come in only infrequently. The attending physician's final conference with the mother was directed toward helping her to understand B's needs and concrete suggestions were made about some ways in which she might help him both in relation to the feeding and other aspects of development. No follow-up is as yet available.

Case 2

A was a white female child known to us from birth until 3 years of age. The family were participants in a longitudinal study of growth and development of children. They were provided with complete pediatric care for the child in return for participation in the study. The following is condensed from a uniquely rich collection of material.

Family history. A was the first-born child of parents in their later twenties, both college graduates. The father was a professional man. For 4 years prior to the pregnancy the mother had combined a full-time business career with marriage. These 4 years of marriage were described as the happiest years of her life. While the parents planned to have children eventually, the pregnancy was unplanned.

They had enjoyed frequent trips and excursions together and the mother anticipated that a child would not only change their mode of living, but would impose new and lasting responsibilities on them. More specifically it meant that the mother would have to abandon her career just as she was about to reach "the top" in her field, because she had firm convictions that a child should be cared for by its own mother and not left to the care of others. She had had no experience with the care of infants. She had a strong preference for a boy and seemed to give little, if any, consideration to the possibility that it might be a girl. Pregnancy, labor and delivery were normal.

Feeding. While feeding was never presented as a major problem, the history of the feeding dramatically illustrates the mother's attitudes toward A and her difficulties in meeting the emotional needs of a young infant.

The patient's birth weight was 2700 gm. She was a full-term, normal infant who sucked efficiently. The mother originally expressed a desire to breast feed but stopped on the fourth day because she feared her breasts would smother the infant. On an evaporated milk formula during the first weeks of life, the patient took 20 to 30 minutes to feed during the day and from 1 to 1½ hours at night, sucking and dozing alternately. The mother expressed annoyance at the length of the early morning feeding as well as the night feedings. By observation it was noted that she fed in a mechanical way, with A laid across her knees and given loose support. While this gave adequate opportunity for sucking, there was no cradling, cuddling or other physical demonstrations of closeness or affection. The mother rarely held or played with her between feedings as she felt A "did not need it" and "it would spoil her." In discussing feeding with the pediatrician, the mother reported ways she had found to shorten the feeding time and lengthen the intervals between feedings. When A was 2 months old the mother discovered that she could take the baby into her bed in the early morning and defer the feeding for a while. During the third month, A was placed almost exclusively in the prone position for sleeping, since in this position she could find her thumb, suck it and go back to sleep for a while longer. During the fourth month the mother reported that A had no tolerance for waiting for food. When she became hungry she would "scream" with great vigor and the mother would "scream back at her."

By 4½ months A had doubled her birth weight and her weight gain and growth were considered adequate. There was no vomiting and no abnormality of the stools at any time. Solids, begun singly in the second month, were taken in small amounts once and then twice daily. By the fourth month the mother asked permission to give solids with *each* bottle feeding so that the interval between feedings could be further lengthened. At 6 months the mother complained that A was no longer interested in eating and was easily distracted by noises and by people. At this time the pediatrician learned through a casual remark by the mother that she had frequently read a book or magazine while she fed the baby.

When the infant was 8 months old the mother began talking to the pediatrician about her own feelings of depression which she felt were out of proportion to the external events. She felt that being a wife and mother gave her insufficient satisfaction and she longed to go back to her work. Her husband often worked late and she missed him very much. On some days she had what she described as "blue spells" when she felt particularly depressed, could not do her housework and occupied herself by reading. On these days the baby seemed a particular intrusion and cried more than on other days. The mother not infrequently reacted to this crying by spanking A as the crying made her feel "wild." She found A a boring and uninteresting companion and consequently rarely played with her. Additionally, she asked "How does one play with a baby, anyway?"

In the home the bathing and dressing were observed to be done efficiently but hurriedly and were almost totally devoid of play. The meagerness of communication between mother and infant seemed to involve all areas of the child's care.

It should be emphasized that the mother gave every evidence of wanting advice and help in the care of her infant and seemed receptive to it. It became increasingly clear that while she could follow suggestions about the techniques of child care, e.g., holding for feeding, she could not supply a positive emotional atmosphere. She went through the motions of caring for her baby, but did this mechanically and without enjoyment. She could not give of herself.

Development. At 8 weeks of age A was normal both physically and developmentally. She was socially responsive, alert and perceptive. She had high visual perception and high social and language responses for her age. Her developmental profile was that of a basically well-endowed infant.

At 3½ months of age (15 weeks) her performance on the developmental examination was normal. Neurologic examination was normal.

From 4½ through 10½ months, A's development became increasingly poor in comparison to her age. At 6 months her development was still within normal limits, but was not as good as it had been earlier. She had relatively poor trunk control and her mastery of large muscle activity was below age. The grasping patterns and other items of fine motor and manipulative skill were slightly above age. Language development which had been one of her highest achievements earlier was now several weeks behind. She was less interested in toys than the usual infant of 6 months, showing no displeasure when they were removed and no real drive to obtain them when they were slightly beyond reach. When they were given to her, however, she demonstrated patterns of adaptation which were fully age adequate. She responded to social stimulation by smiling and initiated a social contact with the adult with a smile of her own. At 9 months the patient's development was at its lowest and most retarded state.

Physical findings. At 9 months of age weight was 6.48 kg (below the third percentile). Height was 67.2 cm (between the tenth and twenty-fifth percentile). She was a small, poorly nourished infant with scanty subcutaneous fat. A papular type rash was present in the genital area; no secondary infection or regional lymphadenopathy was present. Remainder of physical examination, including neurologic and ophthalmoscopic appraisal, was normal.

Laboratory findings. At 9 months of age the concentration of butyl extractable iodine was 5.4 μg/100 ml; erythrocyte count was 5,010,000/mm^3; hemoglobin concentration was 12.0 gm/100 ml; leukocytes were 19,250/mm^3 with 23 polymorphonuclear leukocytes and 76 lymphocytes.

Gesell developmental examination. At the 9-month examination gross motor development was 5 weeks below age. A could sit erect no longer than a minute, was making some efforts to crawl on her belly but could not creep. Fine motor development including all items of prehension, manipulation of small objects and eye-hand co-ordination was age adequate. In adaptive development there were some failures below her age level but a number of successes above her age (one as high as 5 weeks above her age). Language was 11 weeks below her age and was the area of lowest functioning. Her social contacts were weak and poorly sustained and she often reacted negatively to the approach of another person, including her mother. Her interest in toys was desultory and they seemed to give her little satisfaction. The diagnostic impression was that of an emotionally deprived and insufficiently stimulated infant rather than a mentally retarded infant.

Course. During the period from 7½ to 10½ months of age there was growing concern on the part of the staff about prognosis for future development. Further lag in development seemed likely if something more could not be done to help the mother modify her care of A. The mother's attitude toward the developmental lag varied. Initially she was depressed and hopeless and wondered whether or not she should "start over with a new baby" with whom she would have more success. Later she tended to deny that she was concerned.

When A was 9 months of age, the mother, at the pediatrician's recommendation, saw a consultant of wide pediatric and psychiatric experience in the hope that she could be helped to obtain psychotherapy. She spoke to him of her feelings of depression and loneliness and her concern about the infant's development, but expressed the opinion that psychiatrists were for people "who could not help themselves" and not for her.

Efforts by the pediatrician were continued to try to alleviate the crisis for mother and child. Pediatric contacts, which the mother always professed to be helpful, were increased in frequency. It may be that as a result of this the mother was able to follow more of the advice given concerning care and stimulation of the child. She was not able to accept the suggestion that she have part-time help in the care of the baby which would permit her to renew some of the activities outside the home which had been important to her earlier.

Though she spoke wistfully of her career, she felt that she should not turn over the care of her baby to another person even for a few hours a day.

When A was seen at 13 months of age she looked remarkably improved. She could walk with minimal support and crept skillfully. She had made impressive gains in all aspects of development. In the 4 months since the ninth month examination she had progressed 6 months in language development, 5½ months in gross motor, social and adaptive development. Fine motor development which had never been retarded was 1½ months above her age. She now could enjoy and participate actively in a social game with the adult, e.g., a simple ball game. Her level of development in all areas was now age adequate for the first time since she was 6 months of age. The mother's attitude toward the infant had undergone considerable modification. She expressed pleasure that A was now "old enough to understand" and that she could now teach her. An important experience for both was their enjoyment of looking at a picture book together. At 15 months A continued to show improvement. Her developmental progress was evaluated regularly until her third birthday and was normal throughout that period.

Discussion

The syndrome of retarded development in infancy due to insufficient stimulation from the mother or mother substitute must be distinguished from other forms of retardation. Though it is by no means as common as those forms of retardation based on organic disorders or defects, it is of importance because prognosis for future development is good if appropriate therapeutic measures can be instituted.

It must be distinguished from:

1. Those disorders which specifically affect the central nervous system, whether prenatal, natal or postnatal in origin.
2. Retardation secondary to acute or chronic involvement of organ systems outside the central nervous system.
3. Retardation due to infantile psychosis.

Recognition of this disturbance in infants who live in an institution is more common because it has been well documented. Its recognition in the family-reared infant is uncommon. Diagnosis is based upon history and physical examination, findings upon developmental examination, and response to therapy. It is not a diagnosis by exclusion only.

Infants B and A both present the clinical picture of environmental retardation due to insufficient maternal care. It should be emphasized that information leading to this conclusion cannot usually be obtained in a single interview. Even in the case of B, a short-term contact, a series of interviews was required in order to elicit the information. The evidence of a disturbed mother-child relationship was most apparent in the feeding history but the deprivation extended to many other areas of child care as well.

It should be noted that by many standards both of these homes would be described as good homes, and the parents well educated and well read. Each mother's inability to provide an emotional atmosphere that would have fostered her child's development was the result, not of lack of intelligence, but of her psychologic difficulties.

In each of these cases the mother was depressed during a large part of the first year of the infant's life and found no pleasure in meeting the needs of a helpless, dependent baby. One might think of these two mothers as if they were absent from their infants much of the time. Even though they were physically present, their failure to communicate and to stimulate had a depriving effect. In both infants the intake of insufficient food resulted in some interference in growth and nutritional state, the major evidence of which was the slow weight gain from the fifth month on. There was no evidence of avitaminosis or nutritional anemia. Growth in length was within the range of normal for A throughout, and for B for the period in which measurements were taken. Careful physical and laboratory studies revealed no organic disorder. Both infants had elevated leukocyte counts which could not be explained on the basis of evidence of infection. Two of the possible explanations neither of which could be established are infectious lymphocytosis and leukocytosis accompanying pathologic emotional states. Infectious lymphocytosis was described by Smith[6, 7] and of his findings only the elevated white count and relative lymphocytosis were found in these two children. The significance of leukocytosis in emotional states in infancy deserves investigation. Dunbar[8] and Diethelm *et al.*[9] have reported elevated leukocyte counts in adult patients with various pathologic emotional states.

On the developmental examinations, A and B had similar profiles with gross motor, language and social functions showing the greatest depression. In both infants the presence of some problem solving ability and adaptive responses at and above the chronologic age suggested that there was no basic defect in equipment for intellectual functioning. In addition, using the developmental examination as a functional neurologic examination there were no signs of damage to the pyramidal tracts or evidences of damage to the basal nuclei and/or their cortical connections. No localizing neurologic signs were present which might be expressed in defective patterns of grasp, difficulties in manipulation or abnormal movements of the extremities. Responsiveness of all the sensory channels was normal and there was no evidence of cloudiness of sensorium or lack of awareness of the examiner. Evidences of neurologic maturation were present, though some of the patterns were put to minimal use. In addition, the way these infants reacted both to people and to toys suggested a significant disorder in their past experience with people.

The therapeutic environment for this disorder provides positive emotional, social and physical stimulation for the infant. It can be instituted in the hospital setting if adequate personnel is available and the staff is oriented to its importance. Providing a therapeutic environment in the home requires a modification of the parents' attitude and ways of caring for the infant and/or the introduction of a mother substitute who can assume major responsibility for child care. The way in which the pediatrician might work with the family to improve the emotional climate is an important subject, but is beyond the scope of this paper. In rare instances a period of placement in a good foster home may be helpful. Foster home placement is a measure employed with success by child placement agencies for institutional infants showing environmental retardation.

In B the treatment was initiated in the hospital setting. The results were gratifying and improvement was seen surprisingly soon. Often a period of several months in an improved environment is required before major gains can be made.

A's improvement, occurring in her own family, came with a gradual modification in her mother's attitude toward her over a period of time. The mother became able to spend time with A, talking with her and stimulating her. It may be that the pediatrician's continued advice and support were important factors in the change. However, it was evident that the baby's growing older and less dependent was also important. The mother could communicate with, enjoy and stimulate an older infant and toddler in a way that she could not respond to a younger infant. Other factors involved in the modification of attitude and some of the theoretical implications have been discussed by Coleman, Kris, and Provence.[10]

SUMMARY

Case reports of two infants reared in their own families who became retarded developmentally due to inadequate maternal care are presented. Maternal deprivation is one of the causes of retarded development in infancy. The presence of the syndrome in family infants requires emphasis and wider recognition. The differential diagnosis includes retardation due to 1) central nervous system lesions, 2) secondary to acute or chronic involvement of organ systems other than the central nervous system, and 3) accompanying infantile psychosis. Diagnosis is made on history, physical examination, developmental tests and response to therapy. While not a common cause of retardation, its recognition is of importance because prognosis for future development is good if appropriate therapeutic measures can be instituted.

REFERENCES

1. GESELL, A., AND CATHERINE S. AMATRUDA. *Developmental Diagnosis,* 2nd ed. New York: Hoeber, 1954. p. 316.
2. SPITZ, R. A. Hospitalism: An inquiry into the genesis of psychiatric conditions in early childhood. In *Psychoanalytic Study of the Child,* vol. 1. New York: Internat. Univ. Press, 1945, p. 53.
3. LOWREY, L. G. Personality distortion and early institutional care. *Am. J. Orthopsychiat.,* 10:576, 1940.
4. BAKWIN, H. Emotional deprivation in infants. *J. Pediat.,* 35:512, 1949.
5. BAKWIN, H. Loneliness in infants. *Am. J. Dis. Child.,* 63:30, 1942.
6. SMITH, C. H. Infectious lymphocytosis. *Am. J. Dis. Child.,* 62:231, 1941.

7. SMITH, C. H. Acute infectious lymphocytosis; Specific infection; report of 4 cases showing its communicability. *J.A.M.A.*, 125:342, 1944.

8. DUNBAR, H. F. Emotions and Bodily Changes: A Survey of Literature on Psychosomatic Interrelationships, 3rd ed. New York: Columbia Univ. Press, 1946, p. 195.

9. MILHORAT, A. T., S. M. SMALL, AND O. DIETHELM, Leucocytosis during various emotional states. *Arch. Neurol. & Psychiat.*, 47:779, 1942.

10. COLEMAN, ROSE W., E. KRIS, AND SALLY A. PROVENCE. The study of variations of early parental attitudes; a preliminary report. In *Psychoanalytic Study of the Child*, vol. 8. New York: Internat. Univ. Press, 1953, p. 20.

7 & 8

The article "Sociogenic Brain Damage" which was presented earlier discussed the effects of socially disadvantaging conditions on performance on IQ tests. It was made clear that IQ's vary with environmental experience, and two studies involving American Indian children were cited as illustrations of this fact. The papers describing these two studies are reproduced below.

In these papers, "A Study of the Foster Indian Child in the White Home," by Thomas R. Garth, published in 1935, and John H. Rohrer's "The Test Intelligence of Osage Indians," published in 1942, the role that cultural factors play in influencing performance on IQ tests is strikingly underscored.

It is well known that the average performance of American Indians on such tests varies between 75 and 80 points. Garth found that Navaho Indian children raised in White foster homes showed an average increase in IQ test performance of more than 22 points. Similarly, when the discovery of oil on the Osage Indians' land in Oklahoma enabled them to improve their standard of living and to provide their children with a good education, there was a spectacularly dramatic jump in the IQ test performance of the Osage children (which only goes to show how efficiently oil serves to lubricate the neural elements that make for adequate performance on IQ tests).

Findings such as these play havoc with the kind of claims made by Professor A. R. Jensen and others that about 80 percent of IQ test performance reflects genetic determinants, and only about 20 percent environmental influences (Note 1).

The truth is that IQ tests do not measure intelligence as determined solely or even primarily by genes. What IQ tests measure is a result of the interaction of genetic factors with environmental factors such as socioeconomic experience, schooling, emotional experience, and the like. Such tests cannot measure the separate contribution of the many genes that undoubtedly play a role in influencing the development of intelligence because there are, as yet, no known methods of determining in either an individual or a population precisely what the roles of each of these factors or influences may be. It matters not how refined the statistical methods applied to the analysis of the data are, if the data are inadequate or in any way biased, the conclusions drawn from such exercises will invariably be unsound.

NOTE 1: A. R. Jensen, *Genetics and Education* (New York: Harper & Row, 1973), and *Educability and Group Differences* (New York: Harper & Row, 1973). For criticisms of Professor Jensen's position see Carl Senna, ed., *The Fallacy of I. Q.* (New York: The Third Press, 1973); C. L. Brace, G. R. Gamble, and J. T. Bond, eds., *Race and Intelligence* (Washington, D.C.: American Anthropological Association, 1971); Ashley Montagu, *Man's Most Dangerous Myth: The Fallacy of Race,* fifth edition (New York: Oxford University Press, 1974), and "Environment Heredity, and Intelligence," *Harvard Educational Review,* Reprint Series no. 2, 1969.

A STUDY OF
THE FOSTER INDIAN CHILD
IN THE WHITE HOME

Thomas R. Garth

The Binet Intelligence Test was given to eight foster Indian children reared in White homes. When possible the test was also given to the own and foster sibs. The median I. Q. of the foster Indian children was 102.5 with a Q [1] of 4.5. When it was possible to test the own sib and foster sib the mean I. Q. of the former was 75 and the latter the same as the foster child. Few sibs could be found, especially foster sibs. Fourteen Indian orphans being reared in White orphan asylums were tested. The median I. Q. was 86.5 with a Q of 4.9.

Nineteen "Hogan" children (those who live in huts or hogans in

"A Study of the Foster Indian Child in the White Home" by Thomas R. Garth. Reprinted from the *Psychological Bulletin,* vol. 32 (1935), pp. 708–9.
[1 Q represents the symbol for quartile deviation or range.—ED.]

the summer but attend White school during winter) were tested. These had a median I. Q. of 75.3 with a Q of 10.5.

THE TEST INTELLIGENCE
OF OSAGE INDIANS

John H. Rohrer

A. Introduction

Studies of the intelligence of various race groups, through the use of objective tests, have been attempted by two general methods.

The first method is the construction and standardization of tests within a native culture for the purpose of classifying individuals within that group. This type of investigation is exemplified by the work of Leiter (14), Oliver (18), and Mann (15). No such tests have been developed for the American Indian. In any event, this method offers no basis for comparisons between different race groups.

The second method is the application of tests standardized in one culture, to native groups of other cultures. This type of investigation has been used in the studies made on Indian groups in this country, and the general conclusions drawn from these studies are as follows:

(*a*) That the mean intelligence quotient of Indians, as given by the several studies, fall between 69 and 88—as reported by Garth, Serafini, and Dutton (5), Fitzgerald and Ludeman (3), Garth, Schuelke, and Abell (6), Jamieson and Sandiford (12), Goodenough (9), and Telford (22);

"The Test Intelligence of Osage Indians" by John H. Rohrer. From *The Journal of Social Psychology,* vol. 16 (1942), pp. 99–105. Reprinted by permission of The Journal Press.

This paper is adapted from a thesis submitted in partial fulfilment for the Master of Arts degree, Denver University, 1940.

(*b*) That there is a positive correlation between the degree of white blood of a group and the intelligence test scores of that group —Garth, Schuelke, and Abell (6) report a coefficient of correlation of .42, Hunter and Sommermier (12) report a coefficient of correlation of .51.

Before we can accept these conclusions at their face value, it is first necessary to determine what conditions must be met in investigating race differences, and then to ascertain that these conditions have been fulfilled in the studies from which they were drawn.

Race, as we are concerned with it, is purely an ethnological matter, and as such is independent of cultural or other environmental factors to which the individuals may have been subjected. Therefore, before accepting differences in performance as due to differences in race, we must be certain that no other factors have operated so as to influence differentially the performance of either group. In the particular activity with which we are concerned, namely intelligence test performance, there are a number of non-racial factors which may have exerted such an influence and, unless they are either eliminated or equalized for the groups being compared, the results will not be valid for racial comparison. The most prominent of these non-racial factors are: (*a*) Differences in social and economic status, (*b*) Differences in cultural environment, (*c*) Differences in language, (*d*) Differences in schooling, (*e*) Differences in motivation in the test situation, (*f*) Differences in rapport in the test situation, (*g*) Inaccuracy in Chronological Age calculations, (*h*) Inaccuracy in determination of racial intermixture.

The writer, in reviewing the studies cited above, found that in each study two or more of these non-racial factors had operated. Differences in cultural environment and schooling were common to all. In view of this fact, the results arrived at in the study of these Indian groups, and the soundness of the conclusions drawn may be open to serious question.

The present study was undertaken to compare the test intelligence of the average Indian child with that of the average white child of the same chronological age, and to determine whether a difference in average performance is present which may be attributed to a difference in race. This was accomplished by using an Indian group for whom the environmental conditions were enough like that of the group upon whom the tests were standardized to permit a valid comparison of the results.

The group in this study was the Osage tribe of Oklahoma, a member of the Lower Missouri branch of the Siouan family. As a result of royalties from the mineral rights of Osage County, the economic status of the members of the tribe is at least equal to that of the average white individual. The social status of the Osage, unlike that of other racial minorities in the United States, has not suffered as a result of their not being Caucasian. The comparability of their cultural environment to that of the average white person has been assured by modern business methods, and has been increased by a high degree of amalgamation. The bilingual problem, a characteristic invalidating point in many inter-racial studies, is almost absent. English is the language used by all but the oldest members of the tribe. A ruling of the Office of Indian Affairs to the effect that a child of Osage blood cannot attend Indian schools, but must attend either the public schools or tuition schools, has guaranteed a schooling identical with that of the white child of the community. The writer, in administering the tests, found no difference in rapport or motivation in the test situation, between the white and Indian children tested. As records of degree of Indian blood are kept at the Osage Indian Agency, and births are promptly registered there, the accuracy of this information is guaranteed.

B. Statement of the Problem

1. To determine the general intelligence, as measured by the tests used, of part and full-blooded Osage Indians attending the elementary schools of Osage County, Oklahoma.
2. To determine the coefficient of correlation between the degree of Indian blood and intelligence as shown by the tests used.
3. To compare the test intelligence of the average Indian child with the test intelligence of the average white child, as given in the standardization of the tests used.

C. Methodology

The mental tests used were the Goodenough *Drawing Test of Intelligence* (8), and the Otis *Self-Administering Test of*

Mental Ability for Intermediate Grades, Form A (19). The Otis test was administered in grades four to eight inclusive. The Goodenough test was given to the students in grades one to three inclusive.

The population tested were those children of Osage Indian blood attending the public and parochial schools in urban and rural districts of Osage County, Oklahoma. Two hundred and thirty-five of the total Osage elementary school population of 331 children were tested. Because of the large area of Osage County it was not practical for the investigator to test in all of the outlying schools of the country.

In order to determine whether any obtained difference might be due to superior or inferior schooling, in every school an equal number of white children, serving as a control group, were given the same tests at the same time, as the Osage children.

The birth records and records of the degree of Indian blood were verified at the Osage Indian Agency, Pawhuska, Oklahoma. The writer administered the tests and scored and tabulated the resulting data.

D. RESULTS

1. Results of the Osage Group on the Goodenough Scale

The mean intelligence quotient of the 125 children of Osage blood tested by the Goodenough Scale was found to be 103.8, with a standard deviation of 21.2, and a standard error of the mean of 1.89. Table 1 shows the results in terms of derived intelligence quotients for groups of different degrees of Osage blood.

TABLE 1. THE MEAN INTELLIGENCE QUOTIENT, STANDARD ERROR OF THE MEAN, AND STANDARD DEVIATION OF VARIOUS PER CENT OSAGE BLOOD GROUPS ON THE GOODENOUGH SCALE

	Per Cent Indian Blood	N	Mean IQ	Standard Deviation	SE of Mean
A.	1.56 — 6.25	24	100.6	24.20	5.046
B.	6.25 — 24.9	8	102.0	25.32	9.569
C.	25.0 — 49.9	8	99.5	19.16	7.241
D.	50.0 — 74.9	45	105.2	16.05	2.419
E.	75.0 — 99.9	14	104.8	27.86	7.726
F.	100	26	104.6	16.20	3.240

No significant difference was found between the mean intelligence quotient of any group of any given degree of Indian blood and the mean intelligence quotient of any other group of a different degree of Indian blood. No significant difference was found between the mean intelligence quotient of any of the different Osage blood groups and the mean intelligence quotient of the white groups upon whom the tests were standardized.

2. Results of the Osage Group on the Otis Tests of Mental Ability

The mean intelligence quotient of the 110 children of Osage blood tested by the Otis *Test of Mental Ability* was found to be 100.05, with a standard deviation of 18.0 and a standard error of the mean of 1.71. Table 2 shows the results in terms of derived intelli-

TABLE 2. THE MEAN INTELLIGENCE QUOTIENT, STANDARD ERROR OF THE MEAN, AND STANDARD DEVIATION OF VARIOUS PER CENT OSAGE BLOOD GROUPS ON THE OTIS TEST

	Per Cent Indian Blood	*N*	*Mean IQ*	*Standard Deviation*	*SE of Mean*
A.	1.56 — 6.25	24	100.9	18.15	3.784
B.	6.25 — 12.5	5	95.2	23.69	11.845
C.	12.51 — 50.0	3	102.7	12.94	9.151
D.	25.1 — 50.0	39	100.5	19.69	3.194
E.	50.1 — 99.9	12	103.8	14.63	4.411
F.	100	27	97.8	24.10	4.726

gence quotients for groups of different degrees of Osage blood. As was the case with the Goodenough Scale the group means do not differ significantly from each other or from that of the standardization group.

3. Correlation Between Intelligence and Amount of Indian Blood

In computing the coefficient of correlation between amount of Indian blood and intelligence, an arbitrary interval of one-sixteenth degree of Indian blood was used. The range of Indian blood was from one-sixty-fourth to full-blooded Osages. All children of one-sixteenth Osage blood and less, therefore, were grouped together in the first interval. The last interval contained the group whose degree of Indian blood was greater than fifteen-sixteenths.

The correlation between intelligence, as shown by the Goodenough Scale, and amount of Indian blood was found to be +.01.

The correlation between intelligence, as shown by the Otis *Test of Mental Ability,* and amount of Indian blood was found to be +.002.

4. The Control Group

The mean intelligence quotient of the 125 white children tested on the Goodenough Scale was found to be 102.92, with a standard deviation of 19.9 and a standard error of the mean of 1.78.

The mean intelligence quotient of the 110 white children tested on the Otis Test was found to be 98.05, with a standard deviation of 17.68, and a standard error of the mean of 1.69.

The results of the tests administered to the control group show that there is no significant difference in test intelligence between the mean score of the Indian children and the mean score of the white children in Osage County, Oklahoma. This indicates that any discrepancies between the results obtained in the present study and those of previous studies cannot be attributed to the schooling of the Indian children in this study as being superior to that of the standardization group.

E. CONCLUSIONS

1. The mean intelligence quotient of the younger group of 125 children of different degrees of Osage Indian blood, as measured by the Goodenough Test, was found to be 103.8. The mean intelligence quotient of the older group of 110 children of different degrees of Osage Indian blood, as measured by the Otis *Test of Mental Ability,* was found to be 100.05.

2. There is no correlation between the degree of Osage blood and test intelligence, as measured by the tests used in this study.

3. The intelligence quotient, as measured by the above tests, of the average child of any degree of Osage blood is not significantly different from that of the average white child, upon whom the tests were standardized.

4. The Osage group is socially, educationally, and economically on a par with the average white population of the United States. The fact that the test intelligence of the Osage group is not inferior to that of the white population suggests that the general inferiority of American In-

dians in test intelligence is not due to ethnological but to cultural factors. This of course assumes that no important selective factors have been operating within the Osage group such as to render them different biologically, from other Indian groups.

REFERENCES

1. ARLITT, A. H. On the need for caution in establishing race norms. *J. Appl. Psychol.,* 1921, 5:179–183.

2. DANIEL, R. P. Basic considerations for valid interpretations of experimental studies pertaining to race differences. *J. Educ. Psychol.,* 1932, 23:15–27.

3. FITZGERALD, J. A., AND LUDEMAN, W. W. The intelligence of Indian children. *J. Comp. Psychol.,* 1926, 6:319–328.

4. FREEMAN, F. N. The interpretation of test results with special reference to race comparisons. *J. Negro Educ.,* 1934, 3:519–522.

5. GARTH, T. R., SERAFINI, H. J., AND DUTTON, D. The intelligence of full-blooded Indians. *J. Appl. Psychol.,* 1925, 9:382–389.

6. GARTH, T. R., SCHUELKE, N., AND ABELL, W. The intelligence of mixed blood Indians. *J. Appl. Psychol.,* 1927, 11:268–275.

7. GARTH, T. R., SMITH, W. H., AND ABELL, W. A study of the intelligence and achievement of full-blooded Indians. *J. Appl. Psychol.,* 1928, 12:511–516.

8. GOODENOUGH, F. L. Measurement of intelligence by drawings. Yonkers, N.Y.: World Book, 1926.

9. ———. Racial differences in the intelligence of school children. *J. Exper. Psychol.,* 1928, 9:388–397.

10. ———. The measurement of mental functions in primitive groups. *Amer. Anthropol.,* 1936, 38:1–11.

11. HUNTER, W. S., AND SOMMERMIER, E. The relation of degree of Indian blood to score on the Otis intelligence test. *J. Comp. Psychol.,* 1922, 2:257–277.

12. JAMIESON, E., AND SANDIFORD, P. The mental capacity of southern Ontario Indians. *J. Educ. Psychol.,* 1928, 19:313–328.

13. KLINEBERG, O. Race Differences. New York: Harper, 1935.

14. LEITER, R. G. The Leiter international performance scale. *Univ. Hawaii Res. Publ.,* 1936, Series 13, No. 15.

15. MANN, C. W. A test of general ability in Fiji. *J. Genet. Psychol.,* 1939, 54:435–454.

16. ———. Mental measurements in primitive communities. *Psychol. Bull.,* 1940, 37:366–395.

17. MEAD, M. The methodology of racial testing: Its significance for sociology. *Amer. J. Sociol.*, 1936, 21:657–667.

18. OLIVER, R. A. C. General intelligence test for Africans. Nairobi, Kenya Colony: Government Printer, 1932.

19. OTIS, A. S. Otis Self-Administering Test of Mental Ability. Yonkers, N.Y.: World Book, 1928.

20. PETERSON, J. Basic considerations of methodology in race testing. *J. Negro Educ.*, 1934, 3:403–410.

21. ROWE, E. C. Five hundred forty-seven white and two hundred sixty-eight Indian children tested by the Binet-Simon tests. *Ped. Sem.*, 1914, 21:454–468.

22. TELFORD, C. W. Test performance of full and mixed-blood North Dakota Indians. *J. Comp. Psychol.*, 1932, 14:123–145.

9 We have seen thus far various demonstrations of the ways in which cultural influences, on an individual and on a group level, can affect children's growth and development. In the next selection a situation is described in which a group of children's weight gain was retarded, in spite of additional food rations being offered them, because of a detrimental change in emotional climate.

In "Mental Contentment and Physical Growth" Dr. Elsie M. Widdowson has provided what amounts to an experimental, and what is even better, an unpremeditated experimental demonstration of the power of human environmental factors to affect the mental and physical growth and development of children.

Until the century was quite along in years, the mind-body dichotomy was so prevalent that it was not scientifically respectable to believe that what went on in the mind could possibly affect the body. But with the accumulation of a vast amount of evidence to the contrary and the birth of psychosomatic medicine, the mind-body dissociation has forever disappeared. That such a belief could ever have been held constitutes a tribute to the strength and pervasiveness for some two thousand years of Plato's ideas, for it was Plato who was originally responsible for that dissociation.

In her illuminating report, Dr. Widdowson shows how changes that would hardly appear to be noticeable in the behavior of adults toward children can substantially affect both their mental and physical growth and development.

This article is particularly thought-provoking as it provides insights into the importance of the emotional climate between mother and child in the feeding interaction that consumes such a substantial portion of their time together in the child's early years.

"Mental Contentment and Physical Growth" by E. M. Widdowson. From the *Lancet*, vol. 1 (1951), pp. 1316–18. Reprinted by permission of the author and the *Lancet*.

MENTAL CONTENTMENT
AND PHYSICAL GROWTH

E. M. Widdowson

The observations of Beaumont (1833) on his long-suffering subject, Alexis St. Martin, a Canadian trapper who had had a gunshot wound which resulted in a gastric fistula, showed for the first time "the effect of violent passion on the digestive apparatus." Later, Pavlov (1910), Alvarez and his associates (see Alvarez 1929), and many others have made notable contributions to our knowledge of the effect of the emotions on the processes of digestion. There seems to be no scientific doubt that the secretion of the digestive juices may be induced by pleasurable emotions and inhibited by unpleasant ones. It has also been shown that painful emotions will hinder the movements of the digestive tract and that food may remain in the stomach many hours longer than normal if a person becomes frightened or angry after he has eaten a meal.

Macy and her co-workers (Macy 1942) have made an interesting observation on the same topic, but from another angle. They were carrying out long-term metabolic studies on women during pregnancy and lactation. The mother of one of their subjects died during the investigation, and during the week of emotional disturbance the woman showed a large negative calcium balance in contrast to her positive balance at other times, although she went on eating her usual amount of food. Similar observations have also been made on children (Stearns 1951).

Most people would undoubtedly agree in principle with the recommendation of Harington (1608):

"Use three physicians still; first Doctor Quiet,
Next Doctor Merryman, and Doctor Dyet."

Nevertheless the importance of getting these three wise men to collaborate in nutritional experiments is often neglected or not appreciated, and the following observations show what may happen when due account is not taken of their advice.

Near the industrial town in Germany where our unit had its headquarters in 1948 there were two small municipal orphanages. We may call them for the present purpose "Bienenhaus" and "Vogelnest." Each housed about fifty boys and girls between 4 and 14 years of age; the average age was 8 years 8 months in both homes. These children had nothing but their official rations to eat, and, although these were considerably better than they had been in 1946 and 1947, they were still barely adequate for the children's requirements. The children were below normal as regards height and weight, those at Bienenhaus being a little worse than those at Vogelnest. We decided to follow the heights and weights of all these children by weighing and measuring them every fortnight for a year, during the first half of which neither home would receive any additional food, but during the second six months one of the homes, Vogelnest, would be supplied with unlimited amounts of additional bread, so that all the children could satisfy their appetites to the full. Extra jam would also be provided to spread on the bread, and concentrated orange juice to serve as a drink. Supplementary bread had already been shown to promote excellent growth at another orphanage (Widdowson 1948). During the second six months the children at Bienenhaus would continue to be weighed and measured as before but would receive no additional food. In this way it was hoped to get a direct comparison of the growth-rate of children with and without the additional bread.

The children were weighed naked after emptying their bladders, and the measurements were always made at the same time of day, at least four hours after the last meal.

As the first six months went by it became apparent that the children were gaining weight at very different rates at the two homes. A group of boys and girls of these ages should gain an average of about 1.4 kg. in six months (O'Brien et al. 1941). At Vogelnest the average gain was almost exactly 1.4 kg.; at Bienenhaus the mean gain was less than 0.5 kg.

During the second six months the position was reversed. In spite of the extra food provided for the children at Vogelnest, their average growth-rate was less than it had been during the first six months when no additional food was supplied (fig. 1). At Bienenhaus, on

Fig. 1. Average growth in weight.

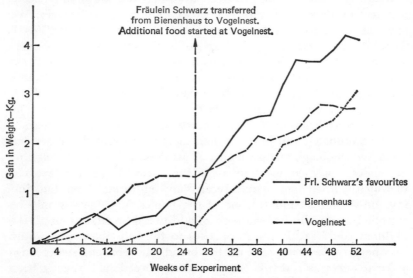

Fräulein Schwarz transferred from Bienenhaus to Vogelnest. Additional food started at Vogelnest.

Gain in Weight—Kg.

Weeks of Experiment

—— Frl. Schwarz's favourites

----- Bienenhaus

– – – Vogelnest

the other hand, the weight curve immediately began to rise steeply, although these children were getting only their German rations as before. There was clearly some other factor at work which was more than counteracting the beneficial effect of the additional food we supplied.

At the beginning of 1948 Bienenhaus was in the charge of Fräulein Schwarz, while Vogelnest was presided over by Fräulein Grün. Just at the time when the additional food was first provided at Vogelnest it so happened that Fräulein Grün left the orphanage to take charge of a children's convalescent home at the seaside. Fräulein Schwarz was thereupon transferred from Bienenhaus to Vogelnest, and a third woman, Fräulein Weiss, came to take charge at Bienenhaus. Fräulein Grün and Fräulein Weiss were very similar in temperament, bright, happy persons, genuinely fond of the children and the children of them. Fräulein Schwarz was quite different. She was older, rather stern and forbidding, and she ruled the home with a rod of iron. Children and staff lived in constant fear of her reprimands and criticisms, which sometimes seemed quite unreasonable. For instance, one day a child was scolded for wearing gloves and getting them wet; the next day the same child was in disgrace for not wearing gloves. Fräulein Schwarz often chose the times when the children were at their meals to administer public rebukes and would single out individual children for special ridicule. The children had to sit in silence while this was going on, with their bowls of soup in front of them. By the time she had finished the soup would be cold; all the children would be in a state of considerable agitation, and several of them might be in tears.

Fräulein Schwarz had her favourites, however, and when she was transferred from one home to the other she persuaded the authorities to allow her to take these eight children with her. These children could do no wrong and they were always assured of praise rather than blame. Their average growth curve has been plotted separately from the others in fig. 1. During the first six months, while they were at Bienenhaus, these children gained more weight than the others in the same home, and from the day they went to Vogelnest and got the additional food they started to put on weight very rapidly, so that in the next six months they gained more than twice the standard amount.

Growth in height did not seem to be subject to emotional influences to such an extent as weight (fig. 2), but the same trends can be seen.

Records were kept of the amounts of food eaten by the children at various stages of the experiment. The calories provided by the German rations were a little higher at both homes during the second six months than the first, probably as a result of the currency reform, and this no doubt partly explains the increased growth-rate at Bienenhaus. But during the second six months the children at Vogelnest were undoubtedly eating more than those at Bienenhaus, and nearly 20% more than they themselves had eaten during the first six months; and yet they failed to put on so much weight.

This kind of experiment is difficult to "repeat" or "confirm," but there is no doubt that even the most perfectly planned nutritional

Fig. 2.　Average growth in height.

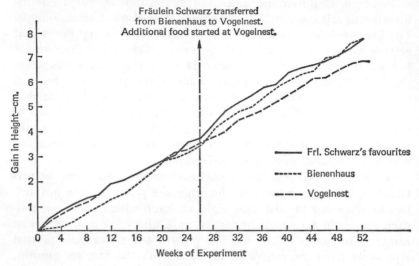

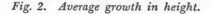

investigation may be ruined by psychological factors over which the investigator may have no control. Those about to embark on feeding experiments would do well to remember "Better is a dinner of herbs where love is than a stalled ox and hatred therewith" (*Proverbs,* xv, 17).

SUMMARY

Work in two orphanages has shown that psychological stresses due to harsh and unsympathetic handling may seriously curtail growth-rates.

REFERENCES

ALVAREZ, W. C. 1929. *J. Amer. Med. Ass.* 92:1231.

BEAUMONT, W. 1833. *Experiments and Observations on the Gastric Juice and the Physiology of Digestion.* Plattsburgh, N.Y.

HARINGTON, J. 1608. The Englishman's Doctor or the School of Salerne. London. Reprinted in *The School of Salernum: Regimen sanitatis Salernitanum.* Edited by F. R. Packard and F. H. Garrison. New York, 1920.

MACY, I. G. 1942. *Nutrition and Chemical Growth in Childhood. Vol. I: Evaluation.* Springfield, Ill., U.S.A.

O'BRIEN, R., GIRSHICK, M. A., HUNT, E. P. 1941. *Misc. Publ. U.S. Dept. Agric.* no. 366.

PAVLOV, I. P. 1910. *The Work of the Digestive Glands.* 2nd ed., translated by W. H. Thompson. London.

STEARNS, G. 1951. *Private communication.*

WIDDOWSON, E. M. 1948. *Brit. Med. J.* 2:104.

10 In the following contribution, "Emotional Deprivation and Growth Retardation Simulating Idiopathic Hypopituitarism," * Dr. G. F. Powell and his coworkers report the clinical findings on thirteen children who were thought to be suffering from inadequate functioning of the pituitary gland (Note 1). Mental as well as physical retardation was present. What in fact these children proved to be suffering from was an inadequate cultural environment. Nutritional deprivation was partially involved. But even more to the point, there was a massive failure to satisfy the emotional needs of these children, with resultant severe mental and physical retardation. Treatment consisted in removing the children to a good therapeutic hospital. No drugs were administered, and no special psychotherapy was provided other than the improved environment. The results of the improved environment were reflected in the improved mental and physical growth of these children.

Unhappily, as only too often happens in cases in which children's health and well-being has been unfavorably affected by the home environment, once the children are restored, to normal growth and development, as in the thirteen cases here reported, they have nowhere to go but back to the home environment which did the original damage, and in which the parents usually resume the torment of the child at the point at which they last left off. It is a tragedy that is repeated an untold number of times in our society every day. Yet our society seems unwilling to acknowledge that the problem exists. It expects that those selfless men and women, social workers, will somehow take care of such difficulties as arise. But, of course, they cannot. Neither institutional care nor social workers constitute answers to a problem of such depth.

There are some individuals who are simply unfitted either for marriage or for parenthood, and it may soon be necessary to consider creating protective legislation in these matters until such time as human beings again become humane and responsible. Until that time we had better begin thinking about the means of making responsible husbands and wives and, in addition, responsible parents.

We do not permit people to drive an automobile or pilot

* By G. F. Powell, J. A. Brasel, and R. M. Blizzard. From the *New England Journal of Medicine*, 276, no. 23, June 8, 1967, pp. 1271–78. Reprinted by permission of the publisher.

a plane without first having demonstrated their ability to do so to a state-appointed board of examiners. The skills required for responsible marriage and parenthood are at least as important to society as the ability to drive a car or pilot a plane safely. We cannot begin thinking about such matters too soon.

Every child who is conceived has a right to be brought into a home in which he or she will be assured of his or her birthright. This birthright consists of the freedom to be born into an environment which encourages one's growth and development, provides one with opportunities to realize one's potentialities to the fullest, and values one's evolution as a warm, loving, humane being. Persons who are incapable of providing the children they conceive with such an environment, or are unwilling to do so, should not be permitted to have children. If this were done, the quantum of misery that now exists in the world would be greatly reduced. Communities would then have an opportunity to focus their attention on what is required to make a healthy human being who can become a healthy parent—who will make healthy children who in their turn will become healthy parents, and make a healthy society.

There is a reluctance to interfere with parents' rights in treatment of their children because of the fear that this would constitute an invasion of privacy, an imposition on democratic privileges. But children are people, too, and they deserve the right to a human and humane existence. Because they are helpless to care for or defend themselves, society *must* make a commitment to protect their right to an environment that supports their optimal development. Upholding the rights of adults at the expense of their children is not democracy; it is a form of slavery. We all have a commitment to children since they are the future of the human race. We must not default on that commitment.

NOTE 1: For those interested, there is a second part of this report, not included here, in which the authors, together with Dr. S. Raiti, provide the endrocrinological evaluation of their findings. For a general discussion of the subject see Lytt I. Gardner, "Deprivation Dwarfism," *Scientific American,* July 1972.

EMOTIONAL DEPRIVATION AND GROWTH RETARDATION SIMULATING IDIOPATHIC HYPOPITUITARISM*
Clinical Evaluation of the Syndrome

G. F. Powell, M.D., J. A. Brasel, M.D.,
and R. M. Blizzard, M.D.

During the past six years we have observed and evaluated 13 children, most of whom initially were believed to have growth failure on the basis of idiopathic hypopituitarism. However, a number of unusual features were noted in the histories that suggested emotional disturbances in the children and abnormal home environments. These were not common to the histories of patients with idiopathic hypopituitarism. When these patients were placed in a convalescent hospital, they demonstrated remarkable growth acceleration without receiving growth hormone or other agents. Detailed studies were performed before and during the period of rapid

* [This paper was generated by] the Department of Pediatrics, Johns Hopkins University School of Medicine and Johns Hopkins Hospital. Supported by a grant (01852) from the National Institute of Child Health and Human Development, National Institutes of Health, United States Public Health Service.

[At the time it was written Dr. Powell was a] fellow in biochemistry research, Department of Biochemistry, Duke University School of Medicine, Durham, North Carolina (supported by a postdoctoral fellowship from the National Institute of Child Health and Human Development). [Dr. Brasel was] assistant professor of pediatrics, Johns Hopkins University School of Medicine. [And Dr. Blizzard was] associate professor of pediatrics, Johns Hopkins University School of Medicine.

[The authors] are indebted to Miss Dorothy Small and Mrs. Bernadine Peters, of the Pediatric Clinical Research Unit, and to the personnel of Happy Hills Home, Baltimore, Maryland, for their assistance in the care of these children, to Dr. Philip Drash and Mrs. Viola Lewis, of the Psychohormonal Research Unit, Johns Hopkins University, who performed the psychologic evaluations, and to Mrs. Mary Westervelt for secretarial assistance.

growth. This paper presents the clinical findings and observations. A subsequent report will detail the endocrine studies and discuss more fully the possible mechanisms for the growth failure.

METHODOLOGY

The patients consisted of 3 females and 10 males (Table 1). Two females (Cases 4 and 6) and 1 male (Case 7) were Negro. After the initial clinical evaluation, all were admitted to the hospital for detailed study, sent to a convalescent hospital for three and a half to twelve months, and readmitted to our hospital for restudy after a period of rapid growth. Observation varied from ten months to six years.

Histories were taken repeatedly from the parents, and supplemented with information obtained by the Social Service and nursing personnel. Laboratory studies obtained were complete blood count, urinalysis and concentration test, serum electrolytes, calcium, phosphorus, alkaline phosphatase, fasting blood sugar, serum urea nitrogen, cholesterol, total protein and albumin-globulin, ratio and five-hour oral glucose tolerance tests (1.75 gm. per kilogram of body weight). In addition, serum carotene was obtained in 9, xylose absorption studies in 5, lipiodol absorption in 2, sweat tests in 3, and stools for ova and parasites in 9. Electroencephalograms were taken in 7.

Radiologic evaluation included a complete bone-age survey before, during and after rapid growth,[1] and x-ray films of the skull and chest. Additional x-ray studies included intravenous pyelography in 3, cinecystography in 1, barium-enema examination in 2, a gastrointestinal series in 2 and pneumoencephalography in 1.

The Wechsler Intelligence Scale for children was performed in 8.

Endocrine evaluation included protein-bound iodine, L-thyroxine (T_4) by column or butanol-extractable iodine determinations, radioactive iodine uptake, water load, ACTH test, metyrapone (Metopirone) test, insulin tolerance tests and growth-hormone determinations on serum obtained during the insulin tolerance tests. Buccal smears were done on the phenotypic females. The endocrine data will be reported in a subsequent paper.

RESULTS

Family History

Cases 6 and 7 were twins, and 1 and 3 were brothers. Otherwise there was no familial history of short stature, endocrine disorder or common disease. There were 1 to 8 siblings, with an average of 4. The position of the patient ranged from first to fourth.

Social histories were similar. Five of the 11 sets of parents were divorced or separated. Marital strife of marked degree was present in at least 2 more sets. Few parents had completed a high-school education, and only 1 of the parents had entered college.

TABLE 1. GROWTH MEASUREMENTS—INITIAL VISIT

Case No.	Chrono-logic Age yr.	Height Age yr.	Bone Age yr.	Actual Upper/ Lower yr.	Expected Upper/ Lower for Chrono-logic Age yr.	Height Age × (100) Chrono-logic Age %	Weight × (100) Weight for Height Age %
1 (Rt.H.)*	3.3	1.8	1	1.27	1.32	53	+15
2 (W.G.)	3.8	2.0	2–3	1.17	1.27	52	−19
3 (Rd.H.)*	4.2	1.2	3	1.25	1.27	30	−20
4 (S.N.)†‡	3.9	2.6	3	1.18	1.25	66	0
5 (G.L.)	4.4	2.0	2	1.26	1.23	45	0
6 (M.P.)*†‡	5.1	2.8	5	1.10	1.19	53	+2
7 (J.P.)*‡	5.1	2.0	2.5	1.22	1.22	39	−13
8 (S.S.)	5.3	3.5	4	1.13	1.19	66	−18
9 (C.W.)	5.8	3.0	4	1.08	1.14	51	−23
10 (G.M.)	6.9	3.5	3–4	1.08	1.10	51	−6
11 (R.C.)†	7.2	4.0	6	1.10	1.07	56	0
12 (G.H.)	7.8	4.5	4	1.06	1.06	60	+7
13 (A.R.)	11.5	5.3	6	1.09	0.98	46	+6

* Siblings (Cases 1 & 3 & 6 & 7 are separate sets).
† Female.
‡ Negro.

Four fathers drank excessively, and 5 were known to be having extramarital affairs. The common pattern was to spend little time at home, and in no case did the father spend much time with the children. All had marked tempers.

Maternal love was more difficult to evaluate. The mothers were interviewed often and provided information about the fathers' behavior but very little about themselves. However, 1 mother stated openly that she hated her son; another was an alcoholic and psychotic.

In 2 cases there were suggestions of gross physical maltreatment of siblings. A sibling of Case 12 was malnourished at four years of age. He reportedly did well in a foster home, when the parents deserted him. A sibling of Case 2 was treated on several occasions at different hospitals for trauma, which probably was inflicted by the parents.

Cases 1, 3 and 9 had siblings of normal height with speech disorders. In only 1 family did siblings of normal stature steal food.

Patient History

In 11 of 13, short stature was the prime reason for referral. Two (Cases 10 and 12) were referred because of behavior problems. One of these (Case 10) was referred for a physical examination before intended placement in a psychiatric institute.

Common features of the history are shown in Table 2. A bizarre type of polydipsia [excessive or abnormal thirst] and polyphagia [excessive or pathological desire to eat] was present in all. Water was drunk from the toilet bowl, glasses filled with dish water, puddles filled with rain water, old beer cans filled with stagnant water and the hot-water faucet. Water was requested frequently during the night. Case 11 had been locked in her room at night to prevent her from repeatedly getting up for water.

According to the history the patients often ate two or three times as much as their siblings at the same dinner table. Examples of aberration included eating a whole jar of mustard or mayonnaise, a package of lunch meat, a whole loaf of bread, corn flour from a box and 7 eggs at 1 sitting. Two ate the food from the cat's dish. Food was frequently stolen. Case 8 stole food from neighbors and a nearby grocery store but never from home. Case 13 hid food in various places throughout the house. Eating from garbage cans was characteristic. Many gorged themselves. Their "stomach would swell," and

TABLE 2. COMMON HISTORICAL FEATURES

Case No.	Polydipsia	Drinking from Toilet Bowl	Polyphagia	Stealing Food	Eating from Garbage Cans	Gorging & Vomiting
1	Present	Present	Present	Present	Present	Present
2	Present	Present	Present	Present	Present	Present
3	Present	Absent	Present	Present	Present	Present
4	Present	Present	Present	Present	Absent	Present
5	Present	Absent	Present	Present	Absent	Present
6	Present	Absent	Present	Present	Present	Absent
7	Present	Absent	Present	Present	Present	Absent
8	Present	Absent	Present	Present	Present	Present
9	Present	Absent	Present	Present	Present	Absent
10	Present	Present	Present	Present	Present	Present
11	Present	Present	Present	Absent	Present	Present
12	Present	Present	Present	Present	Present	Present
13	Present	Absent	Present	Present	Present	Absent

they vomited frequently. Case 13 had abdominal swelling after gorging but no vomiting.

Several children got up at night. This was often to obtain food or water, but a frequent characteristic was to find the children "roaming the house" or "standing looking out the window." Case 11 frequently ran out into the street during the night.

In spite of large families, most of the patients did not join in games and tended to sit and watch the others. Two children are known to have bitten their arms on occasion and drawn blood. Retarded speech was present in 11. This consisted of delayed, immature and indistinct speech. Eight of 13 walked after fifteen months of age.

A history of markedly foul-smelling stools was present in 8. Three of these had a history of bulky stools. Six had had medical evaluation because of these abnormalities. In Case 9 an erroneous diagnosis of cystic fibrosis had been made elsewhere.

Many of these symptoms, including the aberrations of food and water intake, began before two years of age. Onset of symptoms occurred before the second birthday in 8 (Cases 2, 3, 5, 6, 7, 9, 10 and 11). Only Cases 8 and 13 had an onset of symptoms after three and a half years. Case 8 had a sudden onset of symptoms at the age

Getting Up at Night	Playing Alone	Shyness	Retarded Speech	Temper Tantrums	Suggestive Steatorrhea	Encopresis
Absent	Present	Present	Present	Present	Present	Present
Present	Present	Absent	Present	Present	Present	Present
Absent	Present	Present	Present	Present	Present	Present
Absent	Absent	Absent	Present	Present	Absent	Absent
Absent	Present	Present	Present	Present	Present	Present
Absent	Absent	Present	Present	Absent	Present	Absent
Absent	Absent	Present	Present	Absent	Present	Absent
Present	Present	Present	Absent	Present	Absent	Present
Present	Present	Present	Present	Absent	Present	Absent
Present	Present	Absent	Present	Present	Absent	Present
Present	Absent	Present	Present	Absent	Absent	Absent
Present	Present	Absent	Present	Present	Present	Absent
Present	Present	Present	Absent	Present	Absent	Absent

of four years. It should be noted that Cases 4 and 12 were raised by the grandparents for the first two years.

A history of decreased weight for height at some time before being seen was present in all except Cases 4 and 8. Case 4 had a low birth weight, with a normal gestation. All the others had normal birth weights.

Physical Examination

On initial physical examination all were short (Table 1). Height ages were 30 to 66 percent of the chronologic age. Chronologic age when first seen in the clinic ranged from three and three-tenths to eleven and five-tenths years. When the actual weight was compared to the average weight expected for the actual height (eighth column), it was less than expected in 6. Even though these 6 were thin, only 1 (Case 8) appeared malnourished. The upper-to-lower ratio (fifth and sixth columns) was normal for age, as was the dental eruption. The head circumferences were −1 to −11 percent of the average head circumference for the chronologic age and +1 to −9 percent of the average circumference expected for the actual height. All had protuberant abdomens. Some had decreased muscle bulk. Case 5 had a right hemiparesis that was probably secondary to a birth injury. All had depressed or infantile nasal bridges, giving a younger naso-orbital configuration than expected for the age. . . .

Social response was immature, and some of the children were withdrawn. During the initial period of observation there was very little attempt at verbal communication except by Case 8, who conversed freely except when questioned about his home.

Laboratory Data Before Growth Period

Hemoglobins varied from 9.9 to 12.0 gm. per 100 ml., and hematocrits from 32.0 to 40.5 percent. Three had mean corpuscular hemoglobin concentrations below 30 percent. Although the white-cell counts were normal, 5 had eosinophilia (counts of 6 to 23 percent) that was of undetermined origin. The specific gravity of the urine was above 1.024 in all 12 who had concentration tests. All could acidify their urine. There was no proteinuria and no glycosuria, and the microscopical examination of the sediment was negative. Blood chemical findings were normal. The total protein was higher than 5.6 gm. per 100 ml. in the 10 tested. The lowest albumin was 3.6 gm. per 100 ml. The serum urea nitrogen varied from 6 to 19 mg. per 100 ml. Oral glucose tolerance tests were within normal limits in 12 and flat in the other (Case 3). Sucrose and lactose tolerance tests were also flat in Case 3.

The 3 females had normal or near normal bone ages. The remainder (10 males), including the male twin, had retarded bone ages commensurate with their height ages (Table 1). Case 2 had some osteosclerosis, with a coarse trabecular pattern; another (Case 12) had osteoporosis of the pelvis and lumbar spine. Bone films were otherwise normal, and, specifically, there was no evidence of malnutrition. Intravenous pyelograms, cinecystograms, barium-enema study, gastrointestinal series and pneumoencephalograms were all within normal limits.

Serum carotene concentrations were done in 9. Three were less than 70 μg., and 2 were between 70 and 90 μg. (normal, 70 to 200 μg. per 100 ml.). In Case 2, the serum carotene, the xylose absorption and the iodized oil (Lipiodol) absorption were all low; Case 9 had a decreased absorption of iodized oil, but xylose absorption and serum carotene were normal. Xylose tolerance tests gave abnormal results in 2 of 5 others. The stools were negative for ova and parasites in 8 of 9.

The electroencephalograms were minimally and nonspecifically abnormal in 4 of 7. The IQ's were 80 or less in the 8 tested.

Effect of Change of Environment

During the initial hospital evaluation polydipsia, polyphagia and stealing of food either disappeared immediately or persisted for only a few days. A consistent improvement in personality and speech pattern occurred. The children became happier, less withdrawn and far more spontaneous.

Growth Pattern

All gained from 0.9 to 4.5 kg. (2 to 10 pounds) during the initial hospital evaluation. Weight gain continued at the convalescent hospital, and some patients became obese. Case 9, who weighed 23 percent less than expected for height, gained 3.2 kg. (7 pounds) in the first two weeks and continued at a rapid rate until he became obese.

Figure 1 is a composite of the growth rates. In the cases in which early measurements are available, and in the others by extension of the data, growth retardation started at about two years of age, and growth continued to deviate further from normal. Although chronologically eleven months apart, the 2 brothers (Cases 1 and 3) returned to a normal growth rate at the same point in time, while living at home. However, without "catch-up" growth they remained markedly short for age. The older brother was never admitted to the convalescent hospital.

Growth began upon or shortly after admission to the hospital. Growth rates, length of hospital stay and disposition after discharge are shown in Table 3. Rates ranged from 0.5 to 0.8 inches per month, with an average of 0.65 inches per month. The average normal monthly rate for this age range is about 0.20 inches per month. The oldest boy (Case 13) when initially seen was eleven and a half years old, with a height age of five and five-tenths years. Weight was normal for height. During the third month at the convalescent hospital he grew at the fastest rate of all, 1.2 inches per month. Weight gain during the same month was only 0.6 kg. (1.3 pounds), but he

Fig. 1. *Catch-up Growth for the Younger Patients (A), Presented Graphically by the Interrupted Lines, and for the Older Patients (B), Presented Graphically as in A but on a Reduced Scale. Growth during periods in the home is shown by the solid line. Height age is plotted against chronologic age; normal growth is represented by the solid line at 45° angle. The solid line for G.H. (B) that follows the interrupted line represents growth while the patient was in an orphanage.*

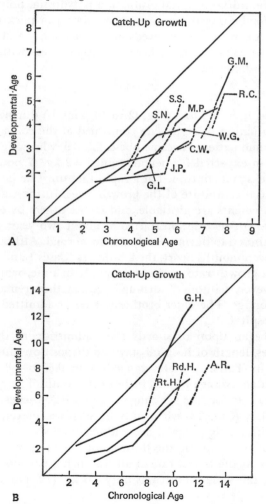

had gained 11.3 kg. (25 pounds) during the two previous months. Case 3, the younger of the brothers, had had a normal growth rate for three years and three months before admission, and the weight was normal for height. Height and weight increased immediately on admission; he became obese, and grew 0.7 inches per month. This increase occurred in spite of the poorest psychologic adjustment of all the children. Although improved, he was hostile, destructive and a difficult management problem during his entire stay. His brother (Case 1) continued growing at home at a normal rate. Consequently, the younger brother became taller (Fig. 1*B*).

The patient (Case 12) who has been followed for the longest time since admission, forty-five months, grew at a maximal rate of 8 inches in the first year. The total increase since admission is 17.4 inches, for an overall rate of 0.39 inches per month. He is now tall and slender and has not entered puberty. At a chronologic age of eleven and a half years, the height age is thirteen years, and the bone age, ten and a half years. Case 10 is the only one who continued to grow at an accelerated rate at home. All the other 7 children (Cases 4, 5, 6, 7, 8, 9 and 11) had a marked decrease in growth rate when discharged. Cases 4, 5, 8, 9 and 11, however, maintained a "normal" or slightly above normal rate. Cases 6 and 7 fell to slightly below a normal rate and lost 0.5 to 0.9 kg. (1 to 2 pounds) in six months. Case 2, who had been discharged to a foster home, grew at a "normal rate" for eight or nine months but then essentially stopped growing. The 3 female patients with normal bone ages on admission still had growth acceleration. One (Case 6) grew at the same rate as her shorter male twin, who had a retarded bone age. . . .

Bone age has paralleled the height increase in Cases 2, 4, 5, 6, 7, 10 and 12. In 3 (Cases 2, 6 and 7), whose growth rate decreased after discharge, the bone age is now greater than the height age.

Discussion

The striking features among these children include the adverse family environment, the bizarre personal history, physical findings simulating idiopathic hypopituitarism and the frequent observation of protuberant abdomens. These features suggest that emo-

TABLE 3. EFFECT OF HOSPITALIZATION ON GROWTH

		Growth in Convalescent Hospital				
Case No.	Duration of Stay mo.	Total Height Increase in.	Increase/ Mo. in.	Total Weight Increase kg.	lb.	Disposition
1 *†	—	—	—	—		—
2	5¾	4.0	0.70	3.55	7.8	Foster home
3*	5	3.5	0.70	4.6	10.2	Still in convalescent hospital
4‡	5	2.75	0.55	1.6	3.6	Home
5	3	1.5	0.50	4.5	10.0	Home
6 *‡	5	4.0	0.80	3.65	8.1	Home
7*	5	4.0	0.80	—	—	Home
8	5	2.5	0.50	6.4	14.1	Home
9	3¼	2.2	0.64	7.67	16.75	Home
10	6	3.75	0.62	8.45	18.5	Home
11 ‡	4	3.0	0.75	5.15	11.3	Home
12	12	8.0	0.66	10.25	22.5	Orphanage
13	10½	6.2	0.58	17.7	39.0	Still in convalescent hospital

* Siblings (Cases 1 & 3 & 6 & 7 are separate sets).
† Not yet admitted to convalescent hospital.
‡ Female.

tional factors, malabsorption, inadequate nutrition and hypopituitarism are possible causes of the short stature.

Although a family history of marital discord, separation or desertion, alcoholism, promiscuity and immaturity is frequent, its occurrence in these cases adds to its importance as an associated or indirect causative factor. Effects of such an environment on child development is complex and has been extensively discussed.[2,3] Short stature may be but one of several consequences of such an environment; others include such disorders as the "maltreatment syndrome," [4,5] failure to thrive,[6] the celiac syndrome,[7] rumination[8] and growth retardation with maternal deprivation.[9,13] The findings in the cases presented were similar to those in these entities.

Evidence for the adverse effect of institutionalization on physical and mental health has been presented in several reports.[12,15] Similar

Follow-Up Period mo.	Total Height Increase in.	Increase/ Mo. in.	Total Weight Increase		Disposition
			kg.	lb.	
		Growth after Discharge from Convalescent Hospital			
21	2.75	0.13	0.7	1.4	Still in foster home
8	2.2	0.27	0.45	0.9	In foster home
4½	1.5	0.33	−1.55	−3.5	Remains at home
7	0.9	0.1	−0.85	−1.9	Remains at home
7	0.65	0.1	0.52	−1.1	Remains at home
2	0.15	0.07	−1.55	−3.5	Readmitted to hospital
10	2.0	0.20	1.2	−2.8	Remains at home
6	2.75	0.46	0.57	1.3	Readmitted to hospital
6½	0.25	0.03	—	—	Remains at home
32	6.75	0.23	3.2	7.0	Still in orphanage

effects occur at home under circumstances of a distorted parent-child relationship.[6,9–11,16–18] The majority of such reports deal with infants, but occasional ones include a more detailed clinical picture in older children.[9,11] The reports on infants have centered on the mother because of her dominant role in child care at this age period. The role of the father has been considered important only in that he has supported the mother. However, an immature father may play a far more important part throughout childhood than previously thought and may account in some way for the large number of males in this study.

The detailed bizarre behavior of these children has not previously been reported with growth failure. Yet it is this bizarre behavior that distinguishes this group of children from those with other types of short stature. Follow-up studies[19,21] of children institutionalized at an early age reveal such deviations as impulsiveness, antisocial and aggressive behavior, low frustration tolerance and lack of normal anxiety. Lowrey[19] studied 25 children, three to four years of age, who had been institutionalized as infants. More than half these children had "hostile aggressiveness, temper tantrums . . . , enuresis . . . , speech defects [varying to near mutism], attention demanding behavior, shyness, and sensitiveness and difficulties about food [refusal, fussy, slow eating, refusal of meat or voracity]. . . ." Seventy percent had speech defects. By contrast, 3 children institutionalized after three years of age did not have these personality disorders. The 2 children in our study without speech defects had onset of symptoms after the age of three years. Severe retardation in language development is one of the most consistent defects noted in various studies of early institutionalization.[20-23]

The behavior of these institutionalized children and the 13 children described here appears to be an aberration of the normal developmental patterns, which usually make their appearance at one or two years of age—that is, speech, feeding oneself, toilet training and initiation of interpersonal relations. In the present study onset of symptoms and growth retardation began at the same time. The first two years of life appear to be most critical in establishing a proper parent-child relationship. Such factors as personal vulnerability and degree or length of disturbance may account for the fact that certain children suffer growth retardation whereas others, including their sibs, do not. These factors need more detailed study.

As previously discussed by Patton and Gardner,[9] psychologic disturbances in the parent-child relationship could account for decreased growth in several ways: failure to provide adequate calories; anorexia, with decreased intake; altered intestinal motility, with decreased absorption; and a direct effect on metabolic processes either at peripheral tissues or centrally in the hypothalamus or hypophysis. The history of polyphagia, poor weight gain, protuberant abdomen and abnormal stools and some of the absorption studies performed suggest that some element of malabsorption may have been present in several children. If present, the defect did not prevent the rapid marked weight gain on admission to the hospital. Present evidence suggests that malabsorption, if present, was mild. More extensive studies on similar patients will subsequently be reported.

Some degree of malnutrition is suggested by the thin habitus and decreased weight for height seen in 6 of the 13 children. The actual caloric intake was impossible to estimate in retrospect. However, all the children were said to have voracious appetites and to eat two or three times as much as their normal siblings at the same table. Although it is impossible to be certain, all indications are that any malnutrition present was not due to inadequate caloric intake. Seven were not underweight for height. Only 1 (Case 8) appeared malnourished. One child (Case 11) immediately stopped growing on discharge from the convalescent hospital when nutrition was adequate (Fig. 1*A*). Other children who were obese had a decrease in growth rate upon being sent home. One would predict that nutritional growth failure would have occurred more gradually. In addition, 1 patient (Case 8) failed to grow normally between hospitalizations although he was overweight for height.

Although a direct psychic effect on growth is suggested by the sudden cessation of growth, the questions of nonabsorption and nonutilization of an essential factor cannot be excluded. Regarding caloric utilization Widdowson[24] indicated the importance of psychologic factors in growth and lack of growth in spite of adequate calories. Others[9,12,18] have observed inadequate growth with adequate caloric intake. Further investigation of nutritional factors, including caloric balance and utilization, is indicated.

In accord with one of the possibilities discussed by Patton and Gardner,[9] evidence that in some cases the reduced growth may result from decreased pituitary function will be presented in a subsequent paper.* The laboratory findings are compatible with diminished somatotropin and ACTH release in the majority of patients studied.

A discussion of physical characteristics, intellectual and speech retardation, catch-up growth patterns and therapy is as important as a consideration of etiology. The decreased head size observed is of some interest since it is of the same degree as that noted in our patients with idiopathic hypopituitarism. The origin of the protuberant abdomen is unexplained, but it may have resulted from decreased muscle tone.

IQ testing was done in 8 children before growth and was 80 or less in all. The children were easily distracted during the test

* [G. F. Powell, J. A. Brasel, S. Raiti, and R. M. Blizzard, "Emotional Deprivation and Growth Retardation Simulating Idiopathic Hypopituitarism: II Endocrinologic Evaluation of the Syndrome, *New England Journal of Medicine,* vol. 276 (1967), pp. 1279–83.—Ed.]

period. This and poor language development may have hampered testing, and the reported IQ's are probably not indicative of capacity. Only repeated testing at intervals will determine whether retardation is due to psychologic problems interfering with testing and whether there has been permanent intellectual impairment. A similar decrease in IQ has been reported to follow institutionalization at an early age.[25]

The accelerated growth rates far exceed normal growth and are similar to the "catch-up growth" rates observed by Prader et al.,[26] Talbot[27,28] and others[29] in patients who were recovering from a number of pathologic states. In earlier studies of maternal deprivation and growth failure similar growth rates were observed with psychosocial therapy.[6,9–11] The periods of accelerated growth were often short, possibly because the children were not removed from their environment. In contrast, our children grew over long periods when removed from their homes. The rapid growth without the administration of exogenous growth hormone and the continued growth during long periods of hospitalization suggests that normal height can be achieved, as it was in Case 12, if inhibitory factors are released or if necessary factors are supplied for growth.

In addition, growth inhibition can persist for many years without permanently suppressing the capacity for catch-up growth (as in Case 13, whose chronologic age was eleven and a half years and whose height age was five and a half years before catch-up growth began). This is in contrast to the suggestion of Patton and Gardner.[9] If skeletal maturation was not delayed to the same extent as the height age, or if skeletal maturation accelerated more rapidly than linear growth, ultimate height would not be normal. Our study provided no evidence that skeletal exceeds linear maturation during the phase of accelerated growth.

Furthermore, the growth observed was unusual in that both acceleration and deceleration occurred rapidly with a change in environment. Possibly, environmental changes occur even within the disturbed homes as evidenced by the simultaneous restoration of the growth rates of Cases 1 and 3 to normal while they were living at home. That this normal growth rate may not be optimum is evidenced by the accelerated and supernormal growth rate of Case 3 when he was removed from the home. His height ultimately exceeded that of his older brother.

Therapy in the present study consisted of placement in a good convalescent hospital. No medications were given, and no effort was made to give these children special medical or psychiatric therapy. This improvement during hospitalization again points up the adverse effect of the home environment and further indicates that separation and deprivation are not equivalent terms. The results suggest that treatment of this type of short stature requires removal from the home until the abnormal parent-child relationship can be improved. Unfortunately, in our cases improvement of the environment has been extremely difficult and without much success. The majority of parents have been uncooperative and have continually failed to show up for appointments. Such failure to improve the environment adequately can be seen from the poor growth on return home.

SUMMARY AND CONCLUSIONS

The present paper explores in detail common features in the family history and aberrations in the personal history of 13 children who had clinical findings suggestive of idiopathic hypopituitarism. These features and findings constitute a syndrome that is common and must be considered whenever short stature is being evaluated. Often detailed and specific questioning may be necessary to elicit the unusual history. The short stature may be but one aspect of a continuum of adverse effects of a distorted parent-child relationship and may be the first suggestion of such a disturbed relationship. Recognition will allow proper treatment and improvement of the distorted relationship and its effects.

Treatment will almost invariably require removal of the child from the home. The help of psychiatrists, psychologists, social workers and other paramedical personnel is essential. In some cases additional assistance from the courts of law is required.

Recognition of the syndrome before placement and subsequent rapid growth will allow detailed investigation of the causative factors, particularly the role of intestinal absorption, nutrition and previous caloric intake. The last will be difficult to document because of the poor reliability of parental histories. Historical features, physical and laboratory findings and rapid growth in an adequate environment should distinguish this syndrome from idiopathic hypopituitarism.

The growth pattern suggests that an adverse environment acting during the early critical years of childhood can be responsible for the growth retardation. Long-term follow-up observation is needed to determine the reversibility of the physical, emotional and intellectual retardation.

References

1. Wilkins, L. *The Diagnosis and Treatment of Endocrine Disorders in Childhood and Adolescence: With the editorial assistance of Robert M. Blizzard and Claude J. Migeon.* Third edition. 619 pp. Springfield, Illinois: Thomas, 1965.

2. World Health Organization. *Maternal Care and Mental Health.* 180 pp. Geneva: The Organization, 1951. (Series No. 2).

3. Child Welfare League of America. Yarrow, L. J. Maternal deprivation. In *Maternal Deprivation: Introduction by Helen L. Wilmer.* 72 pp. New York: The League, 1962.

4. Fontana, V. J., Donovan, D., and Wong, R. J. "Maltreatment syndrome" in children. *New Eng. J. Med.* 269:1389–1394, 1963.

5. McHenry, T., Girdany, B. R., and Elmer, E. Unsuspected trauma with multiple skeletal injuries during infancy and childhood. *Pediatrics* 31:903–908, 1963.

6. Elmer, E. Failure to thrive: role of mother. *Pediatrics* 25:717–725, 1960.

7. Manson, G. Neglected children and celiac syndrome. *J. Iowa M. Soc.* 54:228–234, 1964.

8. Hollowell, J. G., and Gardner, L. I. Rumination and growth failure in male fraternal twin, association with disturbed family environment. *Pediatrics* 36:565–571, 1965.

9. Patton, R. G., and Gardner, L. I. *Growth Failure in Maternal Deprivation: With an introduction by Julius B. Richmond.* 94 pp. Springfield, Illinois: Thomas, 1962.

10. Blodgett, F. M. Growth retardation related to maternal deprivation. In *Modern Perspectives in Child Development: In honor of Milton J. E. Senn.* Edited by A. J. Solnit and S. A. Provence. 666 pp. New York: Int. Univ. Press, 1963. Part 11. Pp. 83–93.

11. Talbot, N. B., Sobel, E. H., Burke, B. S., Lindemann, E., and Kauf-

MAN, S. B. Dwarfism in healthy children: its possible relation to emotional, nutritional and endocrine disturbances. *New Eng. J. Med.* 236:783–793, 1947.

12. BAKWIN, H. Emotional deprivation in infants. *J. Pediat.* 35:512–521, 1949.

13. *Idem.* Loneliness in infants. *Am. J. Dis. Child.* 63:30–40, 1942.

14. FRIED, R., AND MAYER, M. F. Socio-emotional factors accounting for growth failure in children living in an institution. *J. Pediat.* 33:444–456, 1948.

15. GLASER, K., AND EISENBERG, L. Maternal deprivation. *Pediatrics* 18:626–642, 1956.

16. COLEMAN, R. W., AND PROVENCE, S. Environmental retardation (hospitalism) in infants living in families. *Pediatrics* 19:285–292, 1957.

17. PATTON, R. G., AND GARDNER, L. I. Influence of family environment on growth: syndrome of "maternal deprivation." *Pediatrics* 30:957–962, 1962.

18. ENGEL, G. L., AND REICHSMAN, F. Spontaneous and experimentally induced depressions in infant with gastric fistula. *J. A. Psychoanalyt. A.* 4:428, 1956.

19. LOWREY, L. G. Personality distortion and early institutional care. *Am. J. Orthopsychiat.* 10:576–585, 1940.

20. GOLDFARB, W. Effects of psychological deprivation in infancy and subsequent stimulation. *Am. J. Psychiat.* 102:18–33, 1945.

21. BOWLBY, J., AINSWORTH, M., BOSTON, M., AND ROSENBLUTH, D. Effects of mother-child separation: follow-up study. *Brit. J. M. Psychol.* 29:211–247, 1956.

22. RHEINGOLD, H. L., AND BAYLEY, N. Later effects of experimental modification of mothering. *Child Develop.* 30:363–372, 1959.

23. BRODBECK, A. J., AND IRWIN, O. C. Speech behavior of infants without families. *Child Develop.* 17:145, 1946.

24. WIDDOWSON, E. M. Mental contentment and physical growth. *Lancet* 1:1316–1318, 1951.

25. Child Welfare League of America.[3] P.

26. PRADER, A., TANNER, J. M., AND HARNACK, G. A. VON. Catch-up growth following illness or starvation: example of developmental canalization in man. *J. Pediat.* 62:646–659, 1963.

27. TALBOT, N. B. Pediatric frontiers in developmental medicine overview. *Am. J. Dis. Child.* 110:287–290, 1965.

28. TALBOT, N. B. Has psychologic malnutrition taken place of rickets and scurvy in contemporary pediatric practice? *Pediatrics* 31:909–918, 1963.

29. CORDANO, A., BAERTL, J. M., AND GRAHAM, G. G. Growth sequences during recovery from infantile malnutrition. *J. Pediat.* 63:698, 1963.

11 In "Psychosocial Dwarfism: Environmentally Induced Recovery," Drs. John B. Reinhart and Allan L. Drash report the case of a two-egg twin who developed severe mental and physical retardation while her twin brother developed perfectly normally. This case is especially interesting on several scores: first, the girl involved was a dizygotic twin; second, the home environment was far from being the same for her as it was for her brother; third, her parents were well-adjusted individuals; and fourth, neither the girl nor her parents required any treatment other than a change of environment during part of the day in a sympathetic and helpful school.

Once again, in this reading, we observe the case of an apparently constitutionally induced retardation of physical and mental growth which, in fact, proved to be environmentally caused. This case is unusual in the subtlety of both the cause and the remedy. Since she was a twin, one might assume (as her parents did) that her environment was identical to her brother's and that her problem was, therefore, a constitutionally individual one. In fact, although they occupied the same household for most of the same time, the two children clearly did not receive the same treatment. In addition, the girl had been separated from her mother at a time in her life when infants are most susceptible to separation anxiety. The cure in this case was unusual, since the child was not required to leave the situation that had caused her problems. Rather, a change of environment for part of the time, giving her additional attention and the chance to grow, was all that she required.

The change of environment began when Kay was seven years of age, and by thirteen she had caught up to her twin brother in all respects. The assumption that she was constitutionally defective and that her case was "hopeless," as her parents thought, led to the kind of resignation which has in thousands of cases undoubtedly resulted in permanent disability, when nothing more was wrong than the cultural environment in which the individual was conditioned and in which he or she continued to live. These are the sociogenic defectives that we find in many stratified societies, and especially among the poorer classes. Kay's parents were high school

"Psychosocial Dwarfism: Environmentally Induced Recovery" by John B. Reinhart and Allan L. Drash. From *Psychosomatic Medicine*, vol. 31 (1969), pp. 165–72. Reprinted by permission of the authors and Harper & Row, Publishers, Inc.

graduates of the lower middle economic class, but as we have seen in earlier contributions, such retarded children may occur occasionally in the families of the more advantaged classes.

In Kay's case the hostility of her mother played the major role in producing her retardation, once again emphasizing the pivotally important role played by the mother in the growth and development of her child (Note 1).

NOTE 1: For further discussion, with case histories, see R. B. Patton and L. I. Gardner, *Growth Failure in Maternal Deprivation* (Springfield, Illinois: Charles C Thomas, 1963).

PSYCHOSOCIAL DWARFISM
Environmentally Induced Recovery

John B. Reinhart, M.D., and Allan L. Drash, M.D.

A female fraternal twin, who had severe growth retardation beginning in her seventh year, began to recover after entrance into a school environment. Physical, psychological, and social growth was reversed so that, at age 13, she was approximately equal to her twin brother in all respects. Psychosocial factors discovered in retrospect seemed related to recovery and are discussed.

The child who "fails to thrive" frequently presents perplexing problems in both diagnosis and management. Treatment generally has been unsatisfactory. Psychosocial dwarfism due to "maternal deprivation" may be a contributory factor in many of these cases. The syndrome of maternal deprivation dwarfism, long known[1-3] but poorly appreciated in both pediatric and psychiatric circles, recently has received increased attention. Patton and Gardner, in 1963, reviewed studies on the effects of sensory deprivation on physical and intellectual development and presented several new cases.[4] More recently, Powell *et al.* have stimulated increased interest in the syndrome by documentation of an associated, reversible, anterior pituitary deficiency. Following change of environment, they found normal pituitary function and rapid acceleration of linear growth.[5,6]

Powell states that "treatment will almost invariably require removal of the child from the home." Blodgett reported that foster home placement was necessary for improvement in growth in a 4-year-old patient.[7] The experiences of Patton and Gardner were similar.[4] However, in a case of twins with growth failure and rumination, active psychiatric intervention in the family resulted in growth acceleration without removal of the infants from the home.[8]

The present report is of particular interest because physical and developmental recovery was accomplished without disruption of the home or involvement of the parents in formal psychiatric therapy. Developmental acceleration occurred in association with environmental change attendant upon entrance into special education where psychiatrically oriented school personnel provided psychological support and stimulation for the patient and her family.

CASE REPORT

Kay and Tom, twins, were born in April 1954. The gestation was of 9 months' duration and was uneventful except for nausea. The twin birth was unexpected. Kay, the first born, was a vertex delivery, weighing 4 lb. 5 oz. Tom was delivered moments later by frank breech and weighed 5 lb. 6 oz. The twins were considered entirely normal except for low birth weights. The neonatal period was unremarkable. During their first year, the twins remained in good health, and no particular differences in their rates of physical or motor development were appreciated by the parents. At age 10 months, Kay weighed 21 lb. and was 26 in. in length, as compared with her twin brother who weighed 20½ lb. and was 28 in. in length.

At approximately 18 months of age, the twins were noted by the family pediatrician and the parents to be divergent in their rates of development. At age 22 months, Kay weighed 20 lb. 13 oz., and was found to have dry skin and hair. The physician prescribed desiccated thyroid on an empirical basis. However, no appreciable change resulted. Between ages 2 and 4 years, the patient's developmental status became of increasing concern to her parents. In addition to the impairment of physical growth, both motor and vocabulary development were retarded. This was particularly obvious when she was compared with her twin brother who was developing at an entirely normal rate.

At age 3, Kay was hospitalized elsewhere for evaluation. She weighed 18¾ lb. and was 29.8 in. in height. A delay in bone maturation was observed. The other studies were apparently within normal limits. The parents were told that the child was suffering from malnutrition and a nonspecific pituitary disorder. No therapy was recommended. Hospitalizations at another institution followed 6 months later because of further weight loss and dehydration. At that time, her weight was 14½ lb. and her height was 30.5 in. Again, no diagnosis was established and no treatment recommended.

From age 3½ until 7½ years, she remained free of overt illness but gained little weight and grew only 5 in. in height. Developmentally, she remained very delayed. She was refused admittance to school at age 6 because of her short stature and slow mental development. At 7⅓ years, she was tested by the school psychologist and scored 65 on the Binet L-M test and 37 on the Vineland Social Maturity Scale. Her physical measurements at that time were: weight 22 lb.; height 34 in. She was admitted to a class for physically handicapped children.

During the course of her first year in school, a remarkable transformation took place. In 9 months, she grew 5 in. and gained 18 lb. Her intelligence quotient (I.Q.) increased to 93 on the Binet L-M test. She became an active, cooperative little girl who entered happily into school affairs and was quite disappointed to see school come to an end in June. Her appetite and thirst, initially very excessive, returned to normal within the first few months of school.

The teacher and school nurse took a particular interest in Kay. They made special efforts to provide intellectual stimulation and psychological support to which Kay responded eagerly. The comments of the school nurse are particularly pertinent: "When Kay came to our school, she resembled an attractive 3 year old but was actually 7. Her abdomen was large and protruded and she was baby-like in appearance. She was unable to care for herself in the bathroom and unable to walk up an average size step. She had a great tendency to overeat. In the lunch room, she begged food from other children and drank large quantities of water. Frequently, she became ill and vomited because of overeating. Her mother told us that she would eat anything and everything. She seemed to crave all types of food."

Kay was initially seen at our hospital at the end of her first year of schooling. Because of the remarkable physical and intellectual strides that had taken place over the preceding 9 months, it was felt that an extensive evaluation was unnecessary. She was found to be a small but alert 8-year-old child measuring 38 in. in height and 40 lb. in weight. Her bone age was read at $3\frac{1}{2}$ years and her skull X-ray films were considered within normal limits. Routine urinalysis and blood counts were normal. Her protein-bound iodine was 5.9 μg. 100 ml. The physician who initially saw her commented as follows: "This is a very remarkable child in many ways, and we have been particularly impressed with the apparent correlation of growth failure with those factors which retarded her social and intellectual development. The fact that they are related is most apparent from the remarkable growth spurt that she has had in the year in school." *

Kay continued to grow physically at an accelerated rate and improved in her school capabilities. After 2 years in the class for handicapped children, she was transferred to a regular third grade. However, because of difficulty in keeping up, she was transferred quickly to a second grade where she did well. Since that time, she has continued to progress satisfactorily in school both academically and socially. By age 12, she had reached the third perecentile for height and tenth percentile for weight in her age range. Sexual development progressed at a normal rate. She had the onset of menses at age $12\frac{1}{2}$ years.

Kay and Tom were seen again for routine re-evaluation at age 13 years. General examination for both was entirely normal. Kay was $55\frac{1}{2}$ in. tall and weighed 76 lb., as compared with Tom whose height was 58 in. and weight 80 lb. Kay was more advanced in bone maturation with a bone-age reading of $13\frac{1}{2}$ years, compared with $11\frac{1}{2}$ years for Tom. In addition, she was more advanced in terms of

* This patient was seen first at our hospital by Malcolm Holliday, M.D., and Thomas Egan, M.D.

TABLE 1. COMPARISON OF PHYSICAL GROWTH OF TWINS

| Age | Kay | | Tom | |
	Height (in.)	Weight (lb./oz.)	Height (in.)	Weight (lb./oz.)
At birth	—	4/5	—	5/6
3 mo.	20.75	10/4	22	11/10
6 mo.	23	15/6	24.5	16/10
10 mo.	26	20/14	28	20/8
22 mo.	—	20/13	—	—
3 yr.	29.25	18/12	—	—
6 yr.	—	—	43	40
7⅓ yr.	34	22	—	—
8 yr.	38.5	40	48	50
9 yr.	41.0	45	50	56
10 yr.	44.5	50	51.5	58
11 yr.	48.5	58	53.5	61
12 yr.	53.0	70	55.0	68
13 yr.	55.5	76	58.0	80

sexual maturation. Comparison of the physical growth of the twins is presented in Table 1 and is illustrated graphically in Fig. 1.

FAMILY HISTORY

The parents and all living close relatives are in good general health. There is no family history of endocrine or metabolic disease, and no family members have had severe stunting of physical growth. However, several have been at the lower range of normal for adult height. The adult female paternal and maternal relatives are all about 5 ft. in height, while the males vary from about 5 ft. 6 in. to 5 ft. 10 in. The patient has 2 male siblings in addition to her twin, one age 20, the other age 4 years. Both are developmentally and physically normal.

SOCIAL AND PSYCHIATRIC HISTORY

The parents are high school graduates. The mother has worked as a telephone operator, and the father is a white collar worker. Economically, they are in the lower middle income range.

TABLE 2.   COMPARISON OF INTELLECTUAL GROWTH OF TWINS

Age (yr. mo.)	Test	Scores	
		Kay	Tom
6/6	Large Thorndike	—	110
7/5	Binet L-M	65	—
	Vineland	37	—
8/4	Binet L-M	93	—
9/0	CTMM	—	115
9/1	Binet L-M	98	—
11/0	CTMM (language)	82	—
	CTMM (nonlanguage)	89	—
13/3	Binet L-M	93	110
	Jastak (reading)	5.9	10.8
	Grade level	6	8

The parents had lived in the home of the maternal grandmother for several years prior to the pregnancy of the twins. The grandmother had cared for the older son while the mother worked. Early in the current pregnancy, the family moved into a nearby apartment.

The twin pregnancy was quite unexpected but well accepted by the parents. The older son had just entered first grade, allowing the mother more time with the twins. From the beginning, the mother felt that Tom was a more adaptable baby, quiet and easy going, much like his older brother. Kay was quite different—noisier, demanding, not as easy to calm if upset, and cried persistently and steadily if unsatisfied. Also, unlike her brother, she was a rapid eater and did not appear to enjoy cuddling.

A number of "crises," both major and minor, occurred during the twins' first year of life. When they were 4 months of age, their mother sustained a corneal ulceration requiring prolonged patching of the eye and much inconvenience.

At about the same time the father's aunt a person with whom he had always been close, died suddenly. The mother became pregnant again when the twins were 5½ months old. This ended in a spontaneous abortion 3½ months later. During this interval, the maternal grandmother had an exacerbation of a malignancy that rapidly led

Fig. 1. *Comparisons of growth in twins. After 6 years of age, the height of Tom follows the tenth percentile, while weight falls between the tenth and twenty-fifth percentiles for his age range.*

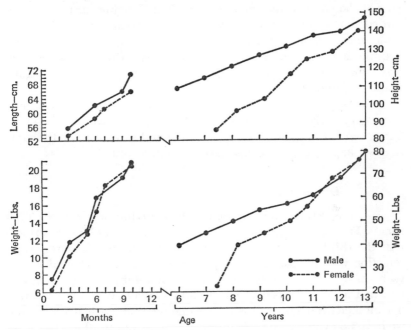

to her death. Her final weeks were spent in the hospital and the twins' mother was occupied continually with her nursing care.

During these various problems, friends and relatives helped out with the care of the twins. Almost invariably, Kay was taken to spend several days with relatives while Tom was left at home with his family. The mother observed that Kay was frequently more difficult to handle after a stay away from home. She became a persistent thumb-sucker, a source of irritation and embarrassment to the mother. Her parents put gloves on her hands "to break her of the habit." "I would never do that again," her mother said. "Kay would fuss and fume about the gloves."

During the twins' second year, a sense of hostility developed between the mother and daughter, clearly recalled by the mother and observed by the pediatrician at the time they became concerned about the child's failure to thrive. Over the next several years, this sense of hostility was replaced by depression and resignation on the part of the parents who came to view their daughter as mentally retarded and destined to be a "dwarf." With entrance into school and rapid increase in physical and psychological growth, the parents became more and more hopeful about Kay. After school progress was assured and her growth approached her brother's, Kay and her family did well.

Both the parents and twins underwent extensive psychiatric interviewing recently. There was no evidence of psychopathology present. They were all individually well adjusted and seemed to be functioning as a happy, psychologically sound family unit.

DISCUSSION

Several factors seemed to be contributory in this child's illness. Fries and Woolf,[9] Chess,[10] and Thomas *et al.*[11] have stressed that the child's congenital activity type determines, in part, his interaction with his parents. Our patient was the more difficult of the twins to deal with for she seemed less adaptable, more persistent, and had a lower threshold for stimuli. It may also have been that her mother dealt less well with a daughter than with her sons, but we have no evidence for this point of view. Even so, there was satisfactory interaction between infant and environment for the first 6 months, for there was no history of feeding, sleeping, or other behavioral disturbances, and physical growth was adequate during this time.

With the final illness of the maternal grandmother to whom the mother was the closest of three siblings, and the mother's own miscarriage soon after her mother's death, we would speculate that the mother experienced some depression and thus became less involved with her children. The mother's eye injury and the death of the father's aunt seemed less significant but were "additional straws on the camel's back."

Both mother and father spoke with great feeling about Kay being the twin chosen to be taken to paternal relatives. During the time Kay was 6–8 months old and throughout her second and third year

—ordinarily a time of increased separation anxiety—Kay was taken on visits which the mother resented, and alienation of mother and daughter was apparent to all. In his office notes, the pediatrician had written of Kay, "she seems to have considerable anxiety about her mother and seems to like her father and brother."

The age at which maternal deprivation occurs may be the most significant factor. Those children reported by Spitz,[12] where separation from their mothers occurred at 3 months, were severely retarded in all respects at followup examination. Our patient, whose first 6–12 months were an average, good living experience, grew well then. When her living experience was changed by her mother's depression, her weekend visits with relatives, resulting alienation from her mother, and other contingency factors, she ceased growing as well as her twin, both physically and psychologically. It may be that the adequacy of the mother-child relationship during the first 6–8 months is the reason that reversibility of the process was possible at age 7.

"Object-relationship,"—i.e., the attachment of this infant to a single mothering person—was relatively stable for the first year, but it was not sufficient to withstand the difficulties this mother-child unit had to deal with in the second year. We can only speculate as to why this infant reacted with the symptom of growth retardation rather than some other physical or behavioral symptom. Perhaps the pituitary-cortical axis was her "weakest link" on a constitutional or genetic basis.

Her persistent retardation in reading skills and apparent decreased intellectual abilities compared to her twin could well be a lingering manifestation of inadequate intersensory development and auditory-visual integration. This delay in neurointegrative development can be viewed as secondary to nutritional risk, deficit in mother-child interaction, or a combination of factors as suggested by Cravioto *et al.*[13] and others.

Our patient's polydipsia—as described in the history given by her parents, noted by her pediatrician in his record, and observed and recorded by her teachers—was similar to that described in patients seen by Powell *et al.*[5] Whether or not this was "psychogenic diabetes insipidus" or a true pituitary deficiency cannot be determined. Studies done at age 3 did not confirm the clinical diagnosis, and pituitary extracts given on an empirical basis apparently did not affect her clinical course and were abandoned. Symptoms disappeared as she adjusted in the school situation.

Feelings of helplessness and hopelessness have been recognized as indicating severe disorganization in response to stress.[14,15] This child might well have been confused by her inability to make meaningful and satisfactory communication with her mother; and her parents, too, may well have been equally frustrated. One can speculate that both child and parents felt hopeless and helpless about the situation. As in Engel and Reichsman's[16] infant with the gastric fistula who reflected her feelings of loss with changes in her gastric mucosa, our patient reacted with behavioral changes and diminished growth. We will be interested in this patient's response to separation in the vicissitudes of her future life.

In retrospect, investigation into the psychosocial aspects of this child's problem of growth failure in her third year might have permitted earlier intervention and less serious and prolonged dysfunction. These factors must be considered in any attempt to accurately assess the child who presents as "growth failure."

SUMMARY

A 13-year-old female fraternal twin who had severe growth retardation, beginning in her second year and persisting through her seventh year, began to grow remarkably after entrance into school. Physical, psychological, and social growth was accelerated so that at age 13, she was approximately equal to her twin brother in all respects. Psychosocial factors were discovered in retrospect which may account for the growth responses.

REFERENCES

1. TALBOT, N. B., SOBEL, E. H., BURKE, B. S., LINDEMANN, E., AND KAUFMAN, S. B. Dwarfism in healthy children: Its possible relation to emotional nutrional and endocrine disturbances. *New Eng. J. Med.* 236:783, 1947.

2. FRIED, R., AND MAYER, M. F. Socio-emotional factors accounting for growth failure in children living in an institution. *J. Pediat.* 33:444, 1948.

3. WIDDOWSON, E. M. Mental contentment and physical growth. *Lancet* 1: 1316, 1951.

4. PATTON, R. G., AND GARDNER, L. I. *Growth Failure in Maternal Deprivation.* Thomas, Springfield, Ill., 1963.

5. POWELL, G. F., BRASEL, J. A., and BLIZZARD, R. M. Emotional deprivation and growth retardation simulating idiopathic hypopituitarism. I. Clinical evaluation of the syndrome. *New Eng. J. Med.* 276:1271, 1967.

6. POWELL, G. F., BRASEL, J. A., RAITI, S., AND BLIZZARD, R. M. Emotional deprivation and growth retardation simulating idiopathic hypopituitarism. II. Endocrinologic evaluation of the syndrome. *New Eng. J. Med.* 276:1279, 1967.

7. BLODGETT, F. M. *Growth Retardation Related to Maternal Deprivation in Modern Perspectives in Child Development,* Solnit, A. J., and Provence, S. A., Eds., Internat. Univ. Press, New York, 1963, p. 83.

8. HOLLOWELL, J. G., AND GARDNER, L. I. Rumination and growth failure in male fraternal twins. *Pediatrics* 36:565, 1965.

9. FRIES, M. E., AND WOOLF, P. J. Some hypotheses on the role of the congenital activity type in personality development. *Psychoanal. Stud. Child* 8:48, 1953.

10. CHESS, S. Individuality in children, its importance to the pediatrician. *J. Pediat.* 69:676, 1966.

11. THOMAS, A., CHESS, S., BIRCH, H. G., HERTZIG, M. E., AND KORN, S. *Behavioral Individuality in Early Childhood.* New York Univ. Press, 1963.

12. SPITZ, R. A. "Hospitalism." In *PSA Study of the Child* (Vol. 2). Internat. Univ. Press, New York, 1946, pp. 113–117.

13. CRAVIOTO, J., DELICARDIE, E. R., AND BIRCH, H. G. Nutrition, growth and neurointegrative development: An experimental and ecological study. *Pediatrics* 38:318, 1966.

14. SCHMALE, A. H., JR. Relationship of separation and depression to disease. I. A report on a hospitalized medical population. *Psychosom. Med.* 20:259, 1958.

15. ENGEL, G. L. *Psychological Developments in Health and Disease.* Saunders, Philadelphia, 1962, pp. 174–178.

16. ENGEL, G. L., AND REICHSMAN, F. Spontaneously and experimentally induced depression in an infant with a gastric fistula: A contribution to the problem of depression. *J. Amer. Psychoanal. Ass.* 4:428, 1956.

12 In the following contribution, "Sex, Status, Gender, and Cultural Conditioning," it is shown that many sexual traits which we customarily take for granted as being genetically determined and, indeed, irreversibly or unmodifiably so, are in fact capable of a considerable degree of modification, even reversibility, under the influence of cultural conditioning. While one's biological sex—that is, being of the male or the female sex—is not capable of any form of cultural modification, one's gender —that is, masculinity or femininity—certainly is. To be a male is not the same as being masculine; the one is a genetically determined status, the other is largely a learned role—a role prescribed by the society into which one is born. The same is, of course, true of the female and femininity.

As in the other very different cases described in these readings, there are biological substrates that account for individual *potentialities* for differences in behavioral responses. From a historical point of view we can see how the sexes came to develop socially in different ways and how important cultural pressures have been. We see, also, that when female infants are raised as males in our own society, the outcome illustrates the point that has been stressed throughout this volume, namely, that genetic potentialities are possibilities and, within the range of those possibilities, culture can do virtually anything with them. Such plasticity has a message for us; it is that we are responsible for seeing to it that the impact of the culture on us and on those in our care is productive and not detrimental to full growth and development as a human being—no matter what one's sex, biological or assigned, and no matter what one's gender.

"Sex, Status, Gender, and Cultural Conditioning" by Ashley Montagu. Originally entitled "Is Sexual Behavior Culturally or Biologically Determined?" Reprinted, with revisions, from *Man in Process* (New York: World Publishing Company, 1961), pp. 165–79.

SEX, STATUS, GENDER, AND CULTURAL CONDITIONING

Ashley Montagu

In this chapter I propose to discuss how physical and mental sexual status has developed in human societies.

The status occupied by the individual in any human society is determined by purely cultural factors. Whether it be inherited, acquired, or assigned—and whatever its nature may be, based or not on some natural characteristic—it is the sanction of a *social group* which gives it being. Social status is not something which is innate or organically determined. It is true that organic differences between individuals in any given society may be socially evaluated in such a way as to serve in certain respects to influence the subsequent status of such individuals. In these cases it is always the cultural sanction which is the determining factor; it is not the organic character as such. There have been frequent claims that the so-called "superorganic achievement of man"—namely, his culture—is the one great accomplishment which serves to separate him from the rest of the animal kingdom. But this anthropocentric claim is, upon examination, found to mean no more than that man is an animal characterized by behavior (whether in the form of institutions or conduct) which is apparently more elaborate and complex than that of which other animals are presumed to be capable. The difference is, in reality, one of degree rather than of kind.

Social studies on animal groups other than man have for the most part been limited to the subhuman primates—the chimpanzee, the baboon of South Africa, and the rhesus monkey of India having served as the chief subjects for study.[1] The few studies on the social

[1] For example, Yerkes, R. M. "Social Dominance and Sexual Status in the Chimpanzee." *Quarterly Review of Biology*, 14, 1939 (p. 115); Zuckerman, S. *The Social Life of Monkeys and Apes*. New York: Harcourt, 1932; Marais, E. N. *My*

life of these creatures are extremely illuminating, for they prove
that no matter under what artificial conditions such groups are
studied the mere "accident" of the association of a number of individuals inevitably leads to the development of a series of social situations which may be more or less knit into something of a formal,
though rudimentary, organization in which it becomes obligatory
that each individual conduct himself in definite ways. Zuckerman,
who has written an interesting account of the social life of the baboon in *The Social Life of Monkeys and Apes,* would probably not
agree with this statement, but his own observations, it seems to me,
provide abundant confirmatory evidence in support of its essential
truth. The clear-cut and determinate social relations which Zuckerman has shown to exist, not only between the individuals of the same
family but also between the individuals of different families among
his baboons, indicate the existence of a pattern of behavior which
can in no way be differentiated from human behavior. Zuckerman
has clearly shown that the family basis of baboon society rests on
the dominance of an overlord who gathers a harem of females about
him and keeps all others at a distance—with the exception of an
occasional bachelor who is admitted into his family upon certain
clearly understood terms.

Such conditions are alone sufficient to produce a fairly complex
social situation, and they do. The strongest males in baboon society
determine the status of all other individuals in it by the use of force
and fear. The relations between the strong and the weak, the aggressive and the timorous animals, are of a very definite order, as their
behavior very strikingly demonstrates. This behavior is social behavior in precisely the same way as our own behavior is social behavior, and it is socially determined by sanctions which are made
and maintained by the strong and applied to the weak. When human behavior regresses to this elementary level we call it not baboon

---

Friends, the Baboons. London, 1939; Carpenter, C. R. "A Field Study of the
Behavior and Social Relations of Howling Monkeys." *Comparative Psychology
Monographs,* 10, 1934 (pp. 1–167); Carpenter, C. R. "A Field Study in Siam of
the Behavior and Social Relations of the Gibbon. (Hylobates lar)." *Comparative
Psychology Monographs,* 16, 1940 (pp. 1–212); Washburn, S. L., and DeVore, I.
"The Social Life of Baboons." *Scientific American,* 204, 1961 (pp. 62–71); Kort-
landt, A. "Chimpanzees in the Wild." *Scientific American,* 206, 1962 (pp. 128–138);
Schaller, G. B. The Orang-Utan in Sarawak," *Zoologica,* 46, 1961 (pp. 73–82).

behavior but "fascism," [2] another form of social behavior based on force seized and held in the hands of a few above the heads of the many. But even in monkey societies, as Dr. Abraham Maslow has shown in "The Rôle of Dominance in Social and Sexual Behavior," [3] the proletarians sometimes rebel. This investigator reveals the fact that among rhesus monkeys a tyrannous overlord who maintains his superior status by force of strength may be overthrown and put in his proper place by the simple expedient of the "ganging up" of the weaker animals on the tyrant, who will generally be so severely chastised that he will thereafter keep a respectful distance from each individual member of that gang. When the workers of the monkey world unite they have nothing to lose but their pains!

The behavior of these social groups of monkeys proves that such status as each individual may enjoy is actually produced and maintained by factors of a social nature akin to those which are operative in human societies. Living, as they do, at a far more elementary level than man has lived for, let us say, these last ten thousand generations, and being perfectly adapted to a natural environment which for them has scarcely changed, monkeys have little need of complex social or cultural relationships. It is not, however, that they are incapable of developing them. But such relations as they have developed fully prove—and this is for us the important point—that status among the subhuman primates, even though it is more often than not based on organic characters, physical strength, or dominance, is able to function only if it is socially allowed or, as it were, sanctioned. The parallel between human and monkey societies is a close one, for in both cases the social sanctions in the ultimate analysis rely upon force for their maintenance, and in both societies they may by the same means be modified or canceled. The difference, then, between human and monkey societies would for the most part appear to lie in the degree to which force has been converted into a power for the development and maintenance of social relationships.

[2] Compare Mussolini's conception of the state with the baboon overlord's conception of baboon society: "The foundation of fascism is the conception of the state, its character, its duty, and its aim. Fascism conceives of the state as an absolute, in comparison with which all individuals or groups are relative, only to be conceived of in their relation to the state." Mussolini, B. *The Political and Social Doctrine of Fascism.* London, 1933.

[3] *Journal of Genetic Psychology,* 49, 1936 (p. 261).

Monkey overlords use their power to gratify their immediate desires, human overlords to fulfill both their immediate desires and their remote wants. It is a difference of degree and not of kind.

As in monkey society, so in human society the social status of the sexes is greatly influenced by the physical differences existing between them. The most important of these differences is physical strength, for it is in virtue of this one factor alone that men are able to enforce their will upon a group of individuals who are principally distinguished from themselves by the possession of peculiar primary and secondary sexual characters subserving functions peculiar to one sex alone. The superior physical strength with which the male is naturally endowed is the one factor which has weighted the balance of power in his favor in human as in monkey society. Indeed, in every living society the correlation is so complete that one may lay it down as a general law that, wherever one sex is larger or stronger than the other, the larger or stronger sex will occupy a position of dominance with respect to the smaller or weaker sex. Thus, in those animal groups in which the females are larger than the males, as among certain fishes and insects, the subservience of the timorous male to the dominant female is complete. This elementary fact— the relationship between strength and sexual dominance in human societies—is often neglected or overlooked by those who are inclined to attribute the differences in sexual status to exclusively cultural factors. In human societies the stronger male is able to establish a physical and social supremacy over the female, which is the starting point of that social supremacy of the male that we find in practically all human societies. From such an initial gross mammalian advantage arise the variegated ways in which the social status of the sexes is expressed.[4]

In the past too much importance has been placed upon the role played by physiological differences related to reproduction in determining the status of the sexes or, rather, the universal supremacy of the male. This view was based on the idea that the processes of pregnancy, parturition, and lactation put the female at a disadvan-

[4] See Montagu, A. *The Natural Superiority of Women.* New York: Macmillan, 1953.

tage in contrast to the male. The facts, however, are that in the vast majority of human primitive societies women are not very greatly incommoded *physically* by these processes. It is only when cultural prohibitions exist in relation to them that any disadvantage becomes apparent. Even among the women of our own social group the physical correlates associated with reproduction are in themselves or their effects hardly a handicap in their rivalry with men. In food-gathering cultures, such as those of the Australians or the Bushmen of Africa, the fact that a woman is pregnant or that half an hour ago she may have given birth to a child is generally responsible for no deviation whatever—except the additive one of nursing —from her customary manner of living. It often happens that on the march she falls out, gives birth to her child, catches up with her companions, and carries on as if nothing had happened. Should another child be born to her a little too soon after the last one, it is killed, for now it constitutes a real disability, since under the conditions of a food-gathering existence it is difficult to take care of more than one infant at a time. There must be adequate spacing between children, not alone for this reason but also because the business of raising a child is considered to be a serious matter.

It would be wrong to underestimate altogether such disadvantages as may exist in the case of the female in relation to childbearing as compared to the male, but it is important to understand that, if the female of the species were the more powerful animal, it is almost certain that childbearing would, in all societies, be esteemed yet another of the physical advantages of the dominant female as compared to the submissive male. In this sense it should be clear that the processes associated with reproduction are irrelevant, whereas physical strength is primary in the actual determination of sexual dominance or subservience. Reproduction does not organically constitute a disability; it is only rendered so *culturally*. As Linton has put it:

All societies prescribe different attitudes and activities to men and women. Most of them try to rationalize these prescriptions in terms of the physiological differences between the sexes or their different rôles in reproduction. However, a comparative study of the statuses ascribed to women and men in different cultures seems to show that while such factors may have served as a starting point for the development of a division the actual ascriptions are almost entirely determined by culture.[5]

If the point be grasped clearly that the "starting point" for the original division of the sexes into the dominant male and the subservient female was and continues to be the greater muscular power of the male, it then becomes possible to understand that the original basis of male dominance everywhere is determined by the same single organic factor—an organic factor upon which man proceeds to erect a great cultural superstructure of differences which, universally, he then claims to represent the expression of biological factors. It is this ascription to biological factors of the determinants of the differences between the sexes that we must now examine. If we have not arrived at this point earlier it has been due to the fact that it was felt necessary to make clear what has generally been neglected in the discussion of these matters, namely, that sexual dominance rests upon an organic basis which gives one sex a certain amount of power over another, whether this power be expressed in physical force or in the creation of laws or customs to the advantage of the male and the disadvantage of the female. Perhaps it may be suggested here that the measure of a people's progress in this connection is the extent to which the male has relinquished some of his muscular power over the female.

If, then, sexual dominance may be taken to have its origins in an organic difference between the sexes, it may well be asked whether it is not possible that all or most of the behavioral differences observable between the sexes are not similarly determined by organic factors. Even though our knowledge of all the factors involved is still far from complete, it is nonetheless possible to return an answer to this question in terms of a very high degree of probability.

Let us first briefly inquire into the nature of the physical differences which exist between the sexes. From the anatomical standpoint the sexes are distinguished by one marked characteristic, the essential genital system, and by nothing else—at least, at birth. Subsequently developed physical differences are limited to the primary

[5] Linton, Ralph. *The Study of Man.* New York: Appleton-Century, 1936 (p. 116).

functions of ovigenesis in the female and spermatogenesis in the male, the secondary differences being represented simply by changes in form or in such characters as the distribution of the subcutaneous fat and of the hair. The differences in the genital systems of the sexes, it is obvious, have their being in the furtherance and realization of the function of reproduction, and it is to be noted that all the functions of this system of organs in the sexes operate in the service of this end—that is, in a purely physiological sense. In the female, for example, the pelvic girdle is a very important part of this system of organs. Since it plays a considerable role in supporting the gravid uterus and in giving passage to the child at birth, the female pelvic girdle differs to the extent necessitated by the actual or potential existence of these conditions from the same structures in the male, which, as far as we know, have never yet been called upon to serve in a similar capacity. Structure in each of the sexes is intimately correlated with function. Even so, the differences between the male and the female pelvis are so slight that the expert will be wrong in his sexing of skeletal pelves almost as often as he will be right. The male is structurally organized to produce fertilization, the female to act as host to the developing organism and as its nutritive agent postnatally.

From the standpoint of the zoologist, mankind, regarded as a noncultural animal, is classified into two sexes in virtue of these functions rather than upon the basis of physical characters which normally serve merely as indices of these functions. Apart from the primary sexual characters, such differences as exist between the sexes are, from the standpoint of the zoologist, purely quantitative, being characterized, for instance, by the *intensity* of local hair growth, distribution of subcutaneous fat, deposition of bony material, and the important characters of body weight and body size. These are examples of secondary sexual characters. The primary sexual characters are immediately recognizable in any human group, in children as in adults; the secondary sexual characters become apparent only with the development of adolescence. From the zoological or morphological standpoint these are the only demonstrable differences which exist between the sexes.

It is evident that the primary sexual characters are fundamentally associated with the different roles played by the sexes in reproduction and that the secondary sexual characters are by-products, as it were, of the systems subserving these different roles—the regulators of bone or hair growth, for example, functioning in a different manner in each sex in consequence of the different hormones poured into the blood stream by the glands associated with each of these systems. Apart from these basic differences for which, incidentally, there is some evidence—at least in respect to the development of several of them—that cultural or sexually selective factors have played a part, it is impossible to say whether there exist any other significant differences between the sexes, physical or otherwise, which are in their immediate origins of a "biological" nature. Are there, for instance, any mental differences between the sexes which can be attributed to a fundamental biological or structural difference?

That appreciable mental differences exist between the sexes in every society is a fact which requires no demonstration, but the assumption that such differences are due to innate biological determinants does require demonstration—and this cannot be done. It cannot be done because such differences are usually the result of the interaction between innate and environmental factors. And the environmental factors are chiefly cultural. While there can be little doubt that hormonal differences tend to result in behavioral difference such, for example, as aggressivity, activity, one is hard put to find an innate basis for many of the usual mental or behavioral differences between the sexes. Certainly, there are such innate bases for maternal behavior, which are lacking in the male. Such maternalizing behavior can be produced in wild Norway rats when one gives them an injection of the maternal hormone, prolactin, but similar results have not been obtained in human males. There are demonstrable genetic, physiological, and biochemical differences between the sexes which have a direct influence upon mental functioning and behavior, but all these differences are capable of being powerfully influenced in both their development and expression by cultural factors.

Many mental differences between the sexes that have customarily been attributed to the operation of biological or innate factors can be shown to be largely if not entirely determined by cultural factors. If biological factors are arbitrarily and customarily taken as the pegs upon which to hang such socially determined mental differences, that, too, must be esteemed no less a cultural device than the mental differences themselves. *Mind, it must always be remembered, is a social product; without society there is no mind.* Of a physical, a biological, or a nonsocial mind we know nothing. But before proceeding further let us return to the physical characters. In what follows, an attempt will be made to show that there is reason to believe that some, at least, of these physical characters have, in the case of the female, in large part been brought about by the operation of cultural factors. If we examine, for example, the nature of a character such as the human female breast, we find that in the order of mammals to which man belongs—the Primates—it is really a unique character. Among man's closest relatives in the animal kingdom, the African anthropoids—the gorilla and chimpanzee—even during pregnancy and lactation the breast is not nearly as well developed as it is in the human female. The conclusion would appear to be obvious: If man originated from some apelike stock, then the characteristic form of the human female breast must have developed during some period after the separation of the human stock from the ancestral Primate group. What brought the peculiar human female breast into being we cannot with certainty tell, but it does seem highly probable that a combination of factors was responsible, in which sexual selection played only a small role, if any.[6]

In the same manner was probably produced steatopygy (the excessive deposit of subcutaneous fat in the buttocks), favored by so many widely separated peoples of the Paleolithic and the Neolithic, and which today is still to be found among a very high proportion of the Bushman women of South Africa. Fat as an object of food is highly prized among all primitive peoples, and as a mark of beauty in women is greatly esteemed. Even in our own society flat-chested

[6] Montagu, A. "Natural Selection and the Form of the Breast in the Human Female." *Journal of the American Medical Association*, 180, 1962 (pp. 826–827).

boyish-breasted women are in the esteem of most men to some extent at a disadvantage as compared to the woman showing something of a bosom. In connection with steatopygy it is of interest to recall that in the rococo period, and again in the early 1880's, the bustle found favor with the fashionable world, chiefly, so it is said, because the poet Jean Paul, like Albrecht von Haller before him, had maintained that it gave an appearance different from that of the apes. It has even been suggested that the bustle became popular in Europe because it gave an actual appearance of steatopygy. This may or may not have been the case.

In addition to the factor of natural selection, the possibility remains that the female breast, as well as steatopygy, developed as a result of conscious, artbitrarily determined, socially selective processes favoring the women possessing such appendages. It would hardly seem possible to explain these characters upon any other hypothesis. This being so, we have here positive evidence of the effects of the operation of a cultural preference upon the actual physical form of the female, determining not alone the distribution of the subcutaneous fat but also its local intensity or density, as well as the form of the breasts. This is an important point, for if the frequency with which certain forms of the body appear can be determined by the long-continued operation of cultural factors, it will readily be understood how preferred types of beauty would come to be established by sexual selection over the course of time, according to a definite cultural pattern.

Differences such as the angulation of the upper and lower arms to one another in the sexes are immediately traceable to purely mechanical factors which result from the sexual differences in the form of the pelvis; they need therefore not detain us here. Differences such as have been said to exist in the weight of the brain between the sexes need keep us here for no more time than it takes to state that the functions of the mind are not dependent upon the size or weight of the brain, but are dependent rather upon its cultural organization. Concerning its structural organization and the relation of that organization to function we know virtually nothing. Furthermore, the weight of the brain in relation to total body weight is greater in the female than in the male.

What, however, are we to say of the differences which exist between the sexes in such oft-cited fundamental characters as the blood? Here surely is something which is independent of the cultural factor? As one writer upon this subject has put the matter:

A very remarkable sex difference, and one which in its fundamental importance is not generally assessed at full value, is in the blood. Our blood, as we all know, consists, for the greater part, of the blood fluid "plasma," and the corpuscles (red and white) which float in the fluid, or to put it more correctly are "suspended" in the plasma. The blood has the very important function, on the one hand, of carrying to all parts of our system the material necessary for the life processes, and, on the other hand, of eliminating and passing out waste matter useless to the organs, the products of metabolism. The red corpuscles have also the particular function of adjusting the gas exchange, that is of extracting the oxygen from the air drawn into the lungs, and delivering it to the various organs, a task which they are enabled to perform by reason of their haemoglobin content. The blood of the adult woman by comparison is richer in plasma and in water-content (80:75 per cent) and produces far less red corpuscles (in one cubic millimetre of blood, 4.8:5.3 million), and thereby the haemoglobin content is less (13:14 per cent). It seems that this sex difference becomes especially marked at puberty. This gulf between the sexes cannot be bridged and no further evidence is required to show how extraordinarily important the blood is in the whole life-process.[7]

Strangely enough this unbridgeable gulf turns out, as has many an unbridgeable gulf before it, to be merely another *pons asinorum* to cross, a privilege which is apparently granted only to those who are able. Hemoglobin is a measure of the functional power of the blood, and stands in a very definite relation to the size of the body and the work that that body is called upon to perform. And while these elementary physiological facts have been known and understood for a considerable period of time, no one, it seems, has ever thought of putting them together and examining them closely for whatever light they might be able to shed upon the causes of man's alleged superior amount of red corpuscles and hemoglobin. Yet the evidence has always been available which should have led to the correct explanation. But when anyone is bent on finding differences in

[7] Heilborn, A. *The Opposite Sexes*. London: Methuen, 1923 (p. 38).

support of a theory, he is content to rest upon the discovery and statement of them—the meaning of the differences found being generally predetermined to fit the theory.

Woman is smaller than man and the amount of work done by her body is physiologically absolutely less than that of man. Her lungs are smaller, hence her oxygen-combining capacity is less than that of man, all this in the absolute sense. In relation to her size, however, it is doubtful whether there can be said to exist any significant difference in the relative amount of the hemoglobin in the two sexes. If there does exist a difference in favor of the male beyond the *relative* amount of hemoglobin for body size (and we would expect to find such a difference in our own social group at least), then this difference is most probably to be attributed to factors which are largely social in origin, for we now have very definite evidence that economic and occupational factors have a very significant influence upon such an "unbridgeable" fundamental character as the hemoglobin content of the blood. It has also long been well known that the oxygen-combining capacity of the lungs is greater in athletes than in normal untrained individuals, and that it is less in sedentary men as compared to active men.[8] Many years ago an English investigator, Lloyd Jones, and, following him, Havelock Ellis, showed "that good physique is associated with high specific gravity of the blood, and poor physique with a low specific gravity; the blood of Cambridge undergraduates [being] of very high specific gravity." "This difference," wrote Ellis, "in the quality of the blood of men and women is fundamental, and its importance cannot be exaggerated; although," he added as an afterthought, "it is possible that its significance may be to some extent neutralized by other factors." [9]

What these other factors may have been was never suggested, but the direction has already been indicated here in which they might be sought—and found. To put the matter briefly, the differences in the hemoglobin content of the blood of the sexes is, when the relative somatic differences have been considered, probably determined

8 Dill, David Bruce. *Life, Heat, and Altitude*. Cambridge: Harvard University Press, 1938.

9 *Man and Woman*. London: Methuen, 1926 (p. 271).

by the differences in occupational status or, more definitely, by the economic activities of the sexes in our society. To the same extent, other things being equal, the pulse, respiration, and metabolism are determined by similarly operative cultural factors.

The extreme environmentalists have argued that sex differences in mental functioning are entirely culturally conditioned. This was the position taken by Mathilde and Mathias Vaerting in their famous book *The Dominant Sex* (1923), or rather it was the position attributed to them, although they were actually well aware of the importance of biological factors in influencing differences between the sexes. Their emphasis, however, was so much on what they called the influence of "the sociological factor" in determining sex differences in mentality, behavior, roles and statuses, that their work, especially in Europe, was widely misinterpreted to support the extreme environmentalist view of sex differences. It is a view which, in an age of iconoclasm, was both appealing and compelling, and it is one which particularly appealed to an anthropologist like myself who had become greatly impressed with the power of cultural conditioning to produce the great diversity of manners and customs so widely spread throughout the world. It was not difficult to challenge the traditional view of sex differences as biologically determined. It was not unamusing to be able to show that many of these entrenched beliefs were quite unsound, and one soon became so enamored of the environmental causation of these differences that there was a tendency to become insensible to the facts.

The truth is that there are a great many sex differences in behavior that are attributed to biological factors which are in fact wholly or almost wholly the results of cultural conditioning. There are others which are almost wholly biologically determined, and there are many which represent the expression of the interaction between biological and cultural conditionings. The important thing for us is to recognize these facts, and to understand that whatever the mental and behavioral differences may have as a biological base, they are all capable of being culturally influenced.

We do not inherit primary or tertiary sexual characters of the mind. The mind at birth is largely sexually undifferentiated, but in every known society the process of differentiation is at that time initiated and thereafter consistently maintained throughout the lifetime of the individual. From the appearance of the body the cultural status of the infant is at once determined. By their external genitalia ye shall know them. In our own society, when a child is born bearing the external genitalia of a female it is at once declared to be a *girl*, or if it bears the genitalia of a male then it is declared to be a *boy*. These are formulas which by traditional heredity have assumed the power to bring about the development of individuals according to the terms in which they are strictly and differentially understood by each culture.

Everyone is familiar with the details of the education of boys and girls in our society; how, from the earliest days, the mind and even the body of each sex is formed upon distinctively disparate lines. As a consequence of such conditioning, of cultural differentiation, it is surely not surprising that such marked differences—differences which it has been actively sought to produce—should exist between male and female. It is well known that the boy who has been brought up exclusively in the society of women tends to be very much more feminine than the boy who has been brought up by a father and a mother, while a girl brought up by males tends to be very much more masculine in her ways than a normally brought-up girl.

In recent years the case for the cultural determinance of sexual role behavior has been clinched by the findings of the endocrinologists. In all, at the time of writing (1962), over one hundred cases have been reported of the masculinization of the external genitalia in female infants born of mothers who had been given certain synthetic progestins (hormones) in early pregnancy. In such cases the fusion of the labio-scrotal folds in these infants may be so complete and the enlargement of the phallus so great that the infant is usually identified as a male and raised as such. The result of being reared as a male is to produce an individual who is psychologically, in attitudes and in gender role, in every way a male. Yet such individuals are physically, except for the slight alteration in the appearance of the external genitalia, in every way perfectly normal females.

The brains of such children have been sensitized by the progestins administered to the mother in the direction of masculinity. But making every allowance for this, there remains no doubt that cultural conditioning plays a dominant role in influencing gender development.

Many cases have been reported in the literature, in no way involving pre- or post-natal hormonal interference, in which sex-reassignment of individuals from infancy has resulted in gender roles being completely reversed for the genetic sex with which they are usually associated.[10] Thus, genetic males reared as females develop all the behavioral traits of femininity usually associated with females, while genetic females reared as males develop all the behavioral traits usually associated with males. While there can be no doubt that male and female hormones continue to play a role in the lives of these individuals, the influence of cultural conditioning in producing psychosexual differentiation is so great that, for all practical purposes, the influence of those hormones is held thoroughly under control by the role expectations of the reassigned gender.

As Drs. Money and Hampson write, "It is indeed startling to see, for example, two children with female hyperadrenocorticism in the company of one another in a hospital playroom, one of them entirely feminine in behavior and conduct, the other entirely masculine, each according to upbringing. As a social observer, one gets no suspicion that the two children are chromosomally and gonadally female, for psychologically they are entirely different." [11]

There are now a good many cases on record of psychologically masculinized females who have married normal females, adopted children, and lived perfectly normal lives as the husband and adoptive father of the children in the family.[12] And, as Money and Hampson have shown, gender role and orientation unequivocally

10 R. J. Stoller. *Sex and Gender.* New York: Science House, 1968; John Money and Anke A. Ehrhardt. *Man & Woman, Boy & Girl.* Baltimore: Johns Hopkins University Press, 1972.

11 Money, John, and Hampson, Joan G. and John L. "Imprinting and the Establishment of Gender Role." *A.M.A. Archives of Neurology and Psychiatry,* 77, 1957 (pp. 333–336).

correspond not with biological sex but with the sex of assignment and rearing.[13] There can no longer be any doubt of the dominant role played by cultural conditioning in determining masculinity and femininity.

Margaret Mead in her excellent book *Sex and Temperament*[14] has provided at once the best and the most important illustrations, based on the study of three primitive societies, of the manner in which different cultures group their social attitudes toward temperament or personality. The Arapesh, the Mundugumor, and the Tchambuli of New Guinea each have constructed their own peculiar and, as between themselves, contrasting types of personality for the sexes, illustrating in a most striking fashion how the psyche is irrelevant to and independent of the biological facts of sex gender. Among the Arapesh, Mead found both the men and the women displaying a personality that we from our own cultural standpoint would call maternal in its parental aspects and feminine in its sexual aspects. Among the Arapesh the sexes were trained to be co-operative, unaggressive, and responsive to the needs of others. The idea that sex is a powerful driving force was altogether unknown to this people. Among the Mundugumor, in strong contrast to these attitudes, men and women developed equally as ruthless, aggressive, positively sexed individuals, with the maternal cherishing aspects of personality at a minimum. Both men and women approximated to a personality type that in our culture would be found only in an undisciplined and very violent male.

Neither the Arapesh nor the Mundugumor profit by a contrast between the sexes; the Arapesh ideal is the mild, responsive man married to the

12 Money, John, and Hampson, Joan G. and John L. "An Examination of Some Basic Sexual Concepts: the Evidence of Human Hermaphroditism." *Bulletin of the Johns Hopkins Hospital*, 97, 1955 (pp. 301–319).

13 Money, John, and Hampson, Joan G. and John L. "Sexual Incongruities and Psychopathology: the Evidence of Human Hermaphroditism." *Bulletin of the Johns Hopkins Hospital*, 98, 1956 (pp. 43–47), and "Hermaphroditism: Recommendations Concerning Assignment of Sex, Change of Sex, and Psychologic Management." *Bulletin of the Johns Hopkins Hospital*, 97, 1955 (pp. 284–300).

14 New York: Morrow, 1935.

mild, responsive woman; the Mundugumor ideal is the violent aggressive man married to the violent aggressive woman.[15]

In the third tribe, the Tchambuli, a striking reversal of the sex attitudes of our own culture was discovered to be the rule; here the woman was the dominant, impersonal, managing partner, the man the less responsible and the emotionally dependent person. From these three situations Mead concludes:

If these temperamental attitudes which we have traditionally regarded as feminine—such as passivity, responsiveness, and a willingness to cherish children—can so easily be set up as the masculine pattern in one tribe, and in another be outlawed for the majority of women as well as for the majority of men, we no longer have any basis for regarding such aspects of behavior as sex-linked. And this conclusion becomes even stronger when we consider the actual reversal in the Tchambuli of the position of dominance of the two sexes, in spite of the existence of formal patrilineal institutions.

From observations such as these it should be quite clear that, as Mead remarks, "the personality traits which we have called masculine or feminine are as lightly linked to sex as are the clothing, the manners, and the form of the headdress that a society at a given period assigns to either sex." Masculinity is not a function determined by a particular set of organs but by a particular cultural emphasis or *habitus*. Hence, strictly speaking, there is no equivalence between such concepts as "male" and "man" or "female" and "woman," for with a reversal of dominance a male may take on the mental characters which in other societies are the prerogatives of the woman, and the female the mental characters which in other societies are the privilege of the man.

In the light of such evidence it becomes apparent that with respect to the mental differences between the sexes in any given society we are dealing not so much with the effects of biological factors, as with *cultural determinants*—cultural determinants which derive their force from a social heredity which we conventionally accept as if it were equivalent to what we understand by our organic or physical

---

[15] *Ibid.*

heredity. Traditional thinking here serves to preserve the practices and beliefs, the errors, the prejudices, and the injustices of primordial ages, and by its authority makes certain that whatever changes must take place in our thinking concerning the status of the sexes shall take place slowly. Whatever the origin of these beliefs it is clear that they have too long outlived the conditions which created them.

13 In "Cultural Deprivation: A Clinical Dimension of Education," Dr. Seymour L. Lustman* underscores the importance of the teacher and the school environment in the healthy growth and development of the child. We do not, especially in America, really respect education, and that is one of the reasons we pay teachers so very little: they are paid what we think they are worth. Yet in the healthy society teaching, next perhaps only to parenthood, would be considered the most important of all the professions. Although our schools are full of young people, there are very few who are students or who are interested in the human values of culture. Education is confused with instruction. Instruction is training in the techniques and skills of the three "R's." Education is the training in the science and art of humanity, the trained ability to relate to others in a cooperative, loving, creative manner, and not alone to all other human beings, but to the whole of nature, every part of it, animate and inanimate.

It is science and technology without humanity, knowledge without feeling, that has brought humanity to the sorry pass in which it finds itself today.

Dr. Lustman has many wise things to say about teachers and the education of the child, and above all about the subtle, damaging cultural deprivations the child suffers at the hands of teachers who appear to have no understanding of the delicate creature who has been entrusted during its most critical years to their care.

Capitalizing on the child's internal drive to development our role as teachers should be the development of internal control rather than external regulation. Dr. Lustman's call for the development of new kinds of teachers and new kinds of schools constitutes a challenge to the contemporary conscience which must be taken up if we are ever to bring about a genuine education in this or any other country.

* From *The Psychoanalytic Study of the Child,* vol. 25 (1970), pp. 483–502. Reprinted by permission of Mrs. Katharine Lustman and the editors of *The Psychoanalytic Study of the Child.*

CULTURAL DEPRIVATION
A Clinical Dimension of Education

Seymour L. Lustman, M.D.

If our primary, and presumably most treasured, asset is our children, no one seriously concerned with the future can deny the pivotal role of education. Any multidisciplinary group charged with planning for generations to come, however divergent their initial focus, must inevitably converge on our schools. This is not only "where the children are," but is an enterprise which commands the nation's largest professionally trained group of workers. If we would but permit our economic and technological power to be brought to bear, the ethical imperative for appropriate facilities and settings could be fulfilled easily. As a system, education remains the ideal hub for a network of consultative talent extending to all areas of life. In point of fact, a sound basis for such a substantive network already has been laid. Accordingly, the educational mission—viewed either as a limited or as an extended area—is crucial and urgent by any set of priorities.

Nevertheless, schools are embattled and in disarray; educators are an unappreciated, beleaguered, and underpaid profession; work fatigue, insecurity, frustration, and consequent job change remain inordinately high; and the magnitude and complexity of the tasks at hand are increasing at a disconcerting pace. Criticism of schools, teachers, and teaching has not always been constructive in tone or intent, nor helpful by design. This is increasingly true of the present. It characterized the decade past as the school preempted the center of our political turbulence. Advice and demands, though plentiful, have not always been far-seeing and altruistic—with either children, teachers or their collaborative work in mind. The lack of humility and the frank opportunism on the part of many politicians, parents,

158

students, teachers, and members of the behavioral sciences have been startling as well as offensive.

And yet, even without such issues of self-seeking territoriality, we are faced with an astonishing, almost inconceivable proliferation of perplexing and divergent needs. From day to day we are presented with numerous redefinitions of the goals of education, which have one fact in common—more and more is asked of it. Physical health, mental health, and a multitude of developmental responsibilities formerly believed to be firmly lodged in the home, parents, families, and a host of other societal institutions such as the church, industry, medicine, psychoanalysis, social work, welfare, the law and the police are now considered integral to the province of education. In the stress of events, we have not had time to weigh these institutional alterations in function, let alone time to plan.

Since no solutions are at hand, and there is every reason to anticipate continued pressure and flux, it is unfortunate that the resultant confusion is held forth by many as presumptive evidence of the school's failure. This is grossly in error. It is more likely evidence of a painful and difficult period of transition—one that will continue for some time to come.

I think this state of affairs has been intensified and deepened by a subtle misapplication of political, social, and economic values to some aspects of education. I speak specifically of egalitarianism, which correctly applies to many social, economic, and civil-libertarian issues, but which nonetheless obfuscates individual differences in educational capability and educational need.

The blurring fails to recognize one of the major conflicts within education which echoes our society. I refer to the balance of individuality and sociality. We will one day have to ponder the degree to which our respect and striving for individuality are compatible with, or locked in contentious struggle vis-à-vis, the demands of our particular kind of society with its gamut of contending and militant views.

At the moment, the problem-solving processes (not necessarily planning processes) at the national and institutional level are locked into heroic issues of social need. At the same time, the individual teacher is locked into the individual needs of individual children. The head and the tail are not yet synchronous.

The teacher knows well individual differences of educational capability and need. Yet, it has become difficult to speak of differences without raising the pejorative accusation of "elitism." Nowhere is this clearer than in our university graduate departments of the performing arts, where many students stubbornly confuse "power" with talent, gift, and creativity.

Planning, on an individual or institutional level, demands discourse of the whole range of needs. In the world of the basketball player, a boy who is seven feet tall, gifted, and trained is the "elite." In the world of the race-horse jockey, the same boy is handicapped. I hope that it is possible to discuss such differences, stripped of their contentious social values as judged by different interest groups. I am speaking of innate and experiential resultants as reflected in the sense of individual differences in all of man's biological and psychological characteristics.

I would like to return for a moment to the issue of the tasks of education. If, in addition to the responsibility for cognitive development, we enlarge the school's mandate to include character development, delinquency, drug abuse, sexual enlightenment, and a host of mental health problems—society must assume that task but must maintain a crucial attitude and construct a more felicitous atmosphere in which to work.

The redefinition of education must retain the historic and traditional scope of its mission; it must not distort, destroy, or deflect the teaching profession; it must broaden that profession's knowledge and capability without overwhelming it or rendering it helpless by conflict; and last, although a consortium of local and federal politicians, parents, students, community organizations, behavioral scientists, and well-intentioned laymen may participate, the ultimate control of *educational activity* must reside within the appropriate group —education itself. The teaching profession must be supported and actively helped to make itself attractive as a satisfying career—one that can compete successfully in the recruitment market for talent; one that can hold its practitioners after their training when they are so desperately needed. Professional status must be enhanced, pay increased, and new career patterns as well as new career ladders be created. If this is not done, we will have the poorest qualifications in those situations where the best are minimal standards.

This requires the educator to become a senior partner in a field that requires the broadest definition, even if inclusiveness increases the risk of a platitudinous tone. One such definition of education in schools would include those gifted aspects of art, those scientifically based techniques and sequential procedures—flexibly used—to maximize the probability for human development. This retains cognitive development and specific content, but permits the inclusion of pediatric care, inoculations, repair of teeth, ways of involving parents and the broader community, nutrition, etc., in addition to the usual and new curricular experiences addressed primarily to content. This was part of the planning and part of the impact of "Operation Head Start." This was never intended to be a program *exclusively* concerned with the "cognitimorphism" of children in terms of IQ points. The increase of IQ points with nursery school experience—whatever that means—was documented in the 1930s. It is possible to retain and enhance that goal (cherished by so many), and still address oneself again to the developmental concerns that psychoanalysis has by tradition shared with teachers.

Psychoanalysts have never made "demands" on educators. Their collaboration is an old and fruitful one characterized by mutual benefit. The atmosphere and spirit of that collaboration goes beyond the shared interest in children. It is true that in a substantive sense, from the viewpoint of the educator, psychoanalysis has been helpful. It has presented a theory of normal and deviant psychological development of inestimable value. From the viewpoint of psychoanalysis, it has been encouraged by the old and immediately perceived view of education as an important period and place to minimize or hopefully prevent disordered development. In addition, psychoanalysis has drawn many of its most distinguished members from the ranks of educators.

The attitude of which I speak was described best by Ernst Kris (1948):

. . . the relationship of psychoanalysis to education is complex. In a first approach the inclination may be to characterize it as one between a basic science and a field of application. Psychoanalytic propositions aim at indicating why human beings behave as they do under given conditions. The educator may turn to these propositions in his attempts to influence human behavior. The propositions then become part of his scientific equipment which naturally include propositions from other basic sciences. In any relationship between a more general set of propositions and a field of application outside the area of experience from which these propositions were derived, a number of factors must be taken into account. The more general propositions, in this instance those of psychoanalysis, must be formulated in a way that permits their operation in a field, here that of education. The process of application is likely to act as a test of the validity of the propositions or of the usefulness of their formulation. Hence we are dealing not merely with a process of diffusion of knowledge from a "higher" to a "lower" level, from the "general" to the "applied" field but with a process of communication between experts trained in different skills in which cross-fertilization is likely to occur [p. 622].

I shall not review the history of this common effort—it has been made available many times, in admirable form, by Anna Freud (1931, 1946, 1954), Aichhorn (1925), Bernfeld (1925), and others. An excellent psychoanalytic review has just been published by Ekstein and Motto (1969). The impact on nursery schools as experienced by a leading educator has been detailed by Omwake (1966).

IMPULSE CONTROL

Although there is great merit in conceptualizing the educational process as an integrated unit extending from prekindergarten through the university, I shall restrict my comments to the primary grades. My focus will be on the issue of impulse control since my interests are with those formative and developmental tasks of early childhood most related to the ability to use a school experience, however it is constructed. My conclusions are drawn from many years of intensive observations and consultation to the Yale University Child Study Center Nursery School, four inner-city prekindergarten programs, access to several inner-city primary schools, the analysis of a number of impulse-ridden children, and several research projects on impulsivity in culturally deprived children. Two of these studies have been reported (Lustman, 1966).

It is my impression that the development of impulse control is one of those key developmental syntheses which signifies the presence of the host of other psychic functions necessary to permit school learning. A child must be able to sit still, to attend, ultimately to concentrate for increasing periods of time in order to perceive, receive, organize, retain, recall, and creatively use knowledge. An internal structure must be developed, sustained, and maintained by internal and external forces. It must ultimately be powered by an inner motivation in order to permit the child to replace internal organization for disorganization in class and outside of it. I am not suggesting that the need for external support, appreciation, and narcissistic supplies ever ceases—but inner structure must be there and cannot be substituted by an exclusively external agent. In other words, the presence of the extraordinary developmental feat of inner control of impulse means that the child can probably use a school experience—although adults can then debate the appropriate or relevant content and forms of presentation. Those are problems of a different nature than the inability to use a school experience because of a developmental deficit which must first be remedied.

In those children where this does not come about, or where it only partially occurs, one is left with an impulse-ridden, uncontrolled individual unable to relate to school, and where the probability of severe trouble in adolescence and later life is enhanced. This is clearly related to the vicious cycle of learning problems, rejection by adults, frustration evolving from no significant experience of success, and in some to the sequelae of severe pathology, dropouts, and delinquency. I add delinquency because of the relationship of superego to control of impulse.

Of course, the scale of inner control ranges from its complete absence to its massive presence. The latter is accompanied by loss of spontaneity, restricted creativity, and characterized by the severe constriction and inhibition noted in some middle-class children in school. Both are developmental problems—one too little, the other too much—which do not augur well for a reasonably harmonious life in school and thereafter.

Either extreme can probably occur in any socially defined group because the number of factors feeding into the development of internal control are numerous and interacting. They are both qualitative and quantitative matters. A variety of causally related sequences can precede similar phenomenological behavior.

However, the prevalence of impulse-ridden children in the so-called "culturally disadvantaged" population is impressive enough to warrant the attempt to relate it to factors within this group. This is not to say that it is universal—but it does seem to be the major impediment to teaching and learning in the poverty-ridden segment of our population.

For the psychoanalyst, this is rooted in the idiosyncratic patterns of object relations which occur in the atmosphere of the family, or whatever substitutes for the usual family's child-rearing functions. However, when speaking of families and familial relationships within the so-called culturally disadvantaged population, one must remain quite clear that this is not a homogeneous population. The common element for this categorization is poverty, not family structure. The population shares most aspects of political, social, and economic disadvantage—but family structure, function, and values vary. The primary family unit ranges from intact families (mother, father, and children together) to incredibly disorganized, ever-changing, and tenuous relationships, the variations of which defy easy categorization. Value systems range from middle-class ideals and hopes to no discernible values other than survival. The range of obstacles and handicaps has been eloquently and accurately described elsewhere in our general as well as sociological literature. Poverty needs no review here. However, the quality of object relationships experienced and established in poorly structured or unstructured "families" and "living arangements" is incontrovertibly causally related to impulse control.

The problem of child rearing in this sizable group of people is not yet the responsibility of either educators or psychoanalysts—although both have helped and continue to try to help. It is assumed that our culture, if it is to survive, will make every conceivable effort to cope with, if not solve, the problems of housing, employment, meaningful participation in community life, involving the caretaking person with the child and both with the educative process. The war on poverty has a massive literature that is not the topic of this paper.

For my purposes, I would like first to generalize, for a moment, on the impact that teaching culturally disadvantaged children has on the teachers I have known. Except for the few gifted and extraordinarily committed teachers, the prevalence and unremitting quality of impulsivity, over a period of time, can have a devastating effect professionally and personally. Teachers, as all professionals, tend to judge themselves by the standards of their training as superimposed on their own unconscious motivations for career choice. Some may be unconscious missionaries, but most, at least in part, share a professional identification as an imparter of, or guide to, knowledge. As she is forced into the unhappy role of a disciplinarian, there is a frequent concomitant feeling of an inability to "reach" her pupils. She may begin to question seriously her talents, her training, her vocational choice, and her future. In addition to such professional conflicts, there are deeper inner conflicts which will be stirred or augmented. Similarly, there is constant exposure to the volatile conflicts of parents as well as militant community forces. Little work satisfaction, professional fatigue, and chronicity may conspire to cause withdrawal from the children. Contagion and disorganization of children who are coping—but with emerging and still fluid ego skills—is regressive for them, and the teacher may find herself feeling forced to a partisan protective position. This may result in greater irritability and "scapegoating" of the disruptive children. The class day may degenerate into a fierce, exhausting, inner and outer struggle centered around control—control of herself and of her pupils.

In talking to teachers, particularly the young, idealistic, and inspired teachers, one is impressed with the additional burden they must bear as elements of social, religious, and racial prejudice emerge within themselves, their colleagues, students, parents, the administration, and community organizations.

In such a crucible, projection as a defense is common. The original challenge and desire to help is in danger of being replaced by a view of her students as having lamentable aberrations to ultimately attributing malevolence to the impulse-ridden child.

Within the first three grades many teachers experience profound relief when these matters are discussed. Insight into the superficial aspects of their own conflicts as well as some understanding of the developmental aspects of impulse control can be helpful. Nevertheless, I have not been impressed by the overall effect of the teacher's greater tolerance, understanding, and comfort on the child's impulse disorder. This is not the case with middle-class children, who are markedly affected by such changes in the teacher.

There seems to me to be a marked difference between the impulsivity of the culturally deprived nursery school child and that of the middle-class child, a difference that goes beyond the higher incidence. In the middle-class child who has a true impulse disorder, there always seem to be elements of object relatedness in the behavior. This usually takes the form of some manipulativeness and elements of a power struggle reminiscent of the earlier anal development. The impulsive behavior is, even though uncontrolled, channeled to some degree into meaningful and communicative behavior, in part directed to the teacher, in part displaced onto the teacher, and always onto the parents. This is quite understandable to most teachers and can be handled effectively and helpfully by many.

The deprived group is more immature. Their behavior is less manipulative, less directed, less communicative, and more unfocused. It seems to be more random, frequently purposeless, and characterized by greater distractibility. Inanimate and human objects are rarely used appropriately for any period of time. Behavior occurs more like constant motion with diffuse generalized bursts of activity best described as a "collective monologue" of behavior similar to Piaget's (1923) collective monologue of speech. It glances off toys, other children, and rarely the teacher—but has almost nothing to do with the teacher (whose name the child may not know). The presence or absence of the teacher has no demonstrable effect on the behavior. However, the strains are so great that the teacher may superimpose an attribute of "badness" on the child which is at least comprehensible, even if incorrect.

In this setting, the teacher becomes deprived, the children's actual and potential deprivation is increased, and an inexorable process of disenchantment and debilitation may ensue for all.

However, the damage to the child is unique for it may be the last opportunity to set in motion the developmental forces he so desperately needs. This can be placed within the context of the psychoanalytic theory of development, but more than that, within a "psychoanalytic learning theory." Such a learning theory would be fundamentally very different from that variety of learning theory which has preoccupied American academic psychology. Except for the largely forgotten Gestalt psychologists, and individuals like Lewin and Piaget, the theories are behaviorist and lean heavily on conditioning paradigms. They are being promoted very earnestly for school use in the form of operant models, machine teaching, and "programmed learning."

To my mind, such theories are not "incorrect" in the sense that man cannot be conditioned—obviously some things can be "learned" via this mode. The error lies in assuming that conditioning is the *only* or even a basic mechanism by which man learns. It reduces man's great gift—his ability to learn—to a mindless response. It leads to such remarkably simplistic and inconsequential theory building as Skinner's (1957) account of the human acquisition of language. The pitfalls of behaviorism have been discussed by Chomsky (1959), von Bertalanffy (1967), Simpson (1967), and Koestler (1967), to name but a few. The reasons for its persistent interest among parents and some educators lie beyond the scope of this paper.

The danger is not theoretical, but lies in the educational practices to which it leads. Koestler makes the point that the original anthropomorphism of the rat now leads to a "ratomorphism" of man. Koestler concludes his scathing review by saying, "It is impossible to arrive at a diagnosis of man's predicament—and by implication at a therapy—by starting from a psychology which denies the existence of mind, and lives on specious analogies derived from the bar-pressing activities of rats" (p. 18). Ludwig von Bertalanffy sees the danger as moving toward a sociology of "robot man," constricted by a "behavioral engineering" tantamount to "functional decerebration"—a new fate for man, i.e., "menticide." The pressure for a "national curriculum" rigidly programmed by behavioral engineers would be particularly devastating to the culturally deprived child for whom it seems particularly aimed. The ethics of such applications of social science may be similar to those of the physical sciences, and reminds me of Max Born's (1968) "nightmare" statement. "The political and military horrors and the complete breakdown of ethics which I have witnessed during my lifetime may not be a symptom of an ephemeral social weakness but a necessary consequence of the rise of science. . . . This is no prophecy, only a nightmare" (p. 58). It is not only science that is involved here, but the uniquely American technological imperative.

For me, the replacing by teaching machine, or rigid programmed

reinforcement, of the extraordinary need for intense *human* relatedness is the ultimate deprivation of the culturally deprived. One
must not confuse automatized, mindless behavior for man's ability
to make rational and responsible decisions. One must not tamper
too much, if at all, with the dignity, grace, and creativity of which
man is capable. Certainly not for a seemingly expedient counterfeit
"intelligence." It represents a particular danger when it is seduc-
tively tied into a machine technology and held forth as a simple
technique to increase cognitive content *and* control of behavior—
both major concerns of our troubled society.

There have been relatively few attempts to explicate a psychoanalytic learning theory, although its importance and existence have
always been taken for granted—insight is a learning term (Piers and
Piers, 1965; Ekstein, 1969; an explicit psychoanalytic learning theory was a matter of primary interest to David Rapaport). It does
not concern itself directly with the development of intelligence or
those aspects of human thought subsumed under cognitive development. However, its concepts of primary and secondary process are
important developmental modes of thinking as well as feeling and
behaving. In the main, as related to schools, it is concerned with
those aspects of internalization and psychic structure building related to characterological development. Such a learning theory
would follow an epigenetic schema from direct and immediate in-
stinctual gratification to controlled, delayed, directed, and even symbolic gratifications. Sublimation as a process would be of extreme
importance. It would developmentally relate frustration, or the absence of gratification, to the learning of differentiation. Memory of
gratification-frustration and ability to use secondary process would
be central to the development of reality testing. Insight as a psychoanalytic learning process is related to, but quite different from, its
use in Gestalt psychology. The affective components, progressive internalization and maturity, and the achievement of motivation at a
greater distance from direct gratification are implied in Ekstein and
Motto's felicitous "From learning for love to love of learning"
(1969).

Mastery in repetitious play and subsequent fantasy is of crucial
learning importance to the age group I am concerned with. To the
extent that psychoanalysis would ever concern itself directly with

cognition, there is every reason to believe that it would evolve a theory consonant with the genetic epistemology of Piaget.

For our purposes the prime applicability of this kind of "learning process" is that it occurs only within the framework of incredibly intense human relationships. These are the vicissitudes inherent in the development of object relatedness. Object relations not only are brought about by human need and human development, but also act as the organizers of psychic function and by their phase-specific crises impel further development. Through processes ranging from conscious imitation to unconscious processes of the varieties of identification, they leave their lifelong imprint. If this does not occur at the appropriate time, or in the intense experiential drama of the home (or other caretaking methods), there is scientific warrant to wonder if it can ever be completed. However, if an effort is to be made short of the impossible and impractical foster home concept, one comes to the school and the teacher.

PSYCHOANALYTIC IMPLICATIONS FOR CULTURAL DEPRIVATION

A complex mental function such as internal control of impulse is an astonishing achievement of advanced development signifying delay, thought, binding of energy, reality testing, awareness of self and others, and degrees of empathy and sympathy. It demonstrates the internal presence of moral values, whatever their cultural content, and the ability to experience and use anticipatory as well as retrospective guilt and anxiety in signal form. Although there are many prestages, and all aspects of this do not occur at once, in its synthetic and multiple function aspects it is well established with the appearance of a definitive superego.

Viewed from a structural theory framework, I would think of it as a complex psychic function resulting from a *superordinate* structuralization. It involves a hierarchical stratification of drive derivatives and defenses with both ego and superego elements having, by temporal interaction, intertwined on ever higher levels of function. Cognitive development depends to a significant degree on this prior step. While it is clear that cognitive development and personality development are related, and seem to continue apace, there is no compelling evidence that cognitive development has a major formative and abiding impact on personality. Training in one cannot be expected to have a generalizing effect on the other—although many psychologists make this assumption. For example, studies in the cognitive development of moral values and judgments (Piaget, 1932), while of interest and value in their own right, have no direct correlation with moral behavior or the experience of guilt. As a matter of fact, there is an imposing body of clinical evidence which demonstrates that knowledge of rules and cognitive moral judgments in no way preclude social psychopathy. On the other hand, characterological psychopathy such as impulse disorder always interferes with learning and cognitive development to a greater or lesser degree.

How can psychoanalytic theory and experience continue to be put at the service of educators? I do not believe in "Freudian schools" and I know that there are many individual ways in which to help and areas in which to start or continue such efforts. Obviously, I think the richest and most commanding problem is the area of impulse control and behavioral morality. Not that I want quiet rooms filled with "good" children. Rather it is that I consider inner control, as described, a problem in schools to which psychoanalysis has the most to contribute. It is also a "target" psychic achievement by which to assess many other aspects of the readiness for, or ability to use, a school. To use psychoanalytic propositions calls for the latitude to develop different kinds of schools, teachers, and programs to meet the different *developmental* needs of this large group of children.

For them, the educational experience must attempt to mobilize and capitalize on the internal impetus to development. If one retains as his anchor the central relevant issues of dropouts, delinquency, learning disorders, and psychopathology, he is led to those aspects of development that are mediated via the kinds of learning described above and mediated only through object-related experience.

Predicated on object constancy and intensity of relationship, this process produces and depends on periodic increases in intrapsychic tension which must reach an unbearable intensity—thereby imposing on the child the need for resolution. Without this, there is arrest, fixation, and distorted development.

Via internalization processes, internal structures are built (which are characteristic for the specific object relationship) and enable the child to delay and control his impulsivity. This process includes aspects of the moral development we attribute to the superego. Object constancy and developmental crises are, I suggest, core prerequisites.

As stated above, it is my impression that the degree of disorganization and impulsivity in the culturally deprived population correlates with the degree of tenuous relationship within the family. There are of course more complicated situations in those instances where clear identification processes with impulsive adults are the major causative factor. At any rate, the disorganized poverty family offers no basis upon which to form the kind of object ties needed for the developmental process.

It may prove fruitful to reconstruct the primary school in an ungraded fashion, devoted to overcoming this primary object deprivation and capitalizing on the child's hunger for human objects. This shifts the emphasis to object ties with the teacher rather than cognitive development in terms of content and IQ scores. In this context external regulation may still become internal control.

Under the imperative of a cognitively based curriculum for all, grades are organized by an orderly progression of content, teachers have become specialized by grade and further specialized by content within grade. The idea of compensatory education has resulted, by and large, in the introduction of even more specialization and loss in individually sustained contact. This is clearly valuable for those children who are secure enough in their development to use it, i.e., those with reasonably secure family ties. It is bewildering to the others and may be harmful.

If one decides that the primary need is object relationships, some obvious experiments come to mind. The first problem is to make the teacher *the* crucial, or *a* crucial, person. This calls for small groups of children, and specially selected and trained teachers, amply supported by expert help designed for their needs as well as the children's.

In essence it is an attempt to give the child, via the teacher, what he has never had: a prolonged, consistent, almost exclusive relationship with an adult who cares for him. To bring this about may require the assignment of *one* teacher to teach *all* content herself and to remain with the same small group of children for perhaps eight years. This is in sharp contrast to our current cognitively based educational patterns with their aforementioned specialization. At present, with yearly teacher change, the child is expected to relate to a large number of primary teachers and an infinite number of subject specialists. This is not helpful to the child who has not had the opportunity to invest deeply in one adult, let alone the few inconstant adults available.

Within this framework, a systematic research effort must be made to delineate circumstances and techniques by which the object tie to the teacher can be most rapidly and firmly enhanced. The work of Anna Freud is succinctly applicable, and if I may paraphrase her (1965b), the best interests of the child and the probability of his continued development will be enhanced if *three needs* are fulfilled and safeguarded. First, the need for *affection*. By teacher selection and support, by small numbers, by genuine responsibility, and by long-term proximity, the chance for this may be enhanced. Second, the need for *stimulation*. The committed teacher's ability to elicit inherent functions and potentialities becomes most meaningful under the conditions described. Third, the need for *unbroken continuity*. In part, this is to prevent further damage to and dulling of feelings attendant on separation. However, within this context, it is designed more to encourage the intensity of relationship crucial to *induce* development. It may call for experimentation with periodic introduction of a male teacher or one male-one female team teaching. It would seem probable that within such an extended period of responsibility, "crisis and rescue" situations will occur which will further enhance the object tie. Consistent and prolonged firmness by one teacher may make possible the internalization of benevolent control via identification. In such a program, content would not be ignored, but would aid and be aided by the focus on object constancy, object ties, and intensity of relationship.

CONCLUSIONS

It seems to me that no culture has ever survived with but one kind of institution—any more than it can survive with a "Tower of Babel." An institution has the same basic architectonic principle at work that biology has; i.e., function determines structure. We have been singularly ineffective in the attempt to use the middle-class school structure in culturally deprived areas. We must evolve new kinds of schools and new experiential educational programs for a significant portion of the deprived population. Although deprived in every sense—including cognition—a significant group of this population is deprived in almost all areas of personality development. These children cannot use the middle-class school structure, and they seriously compromise the other children who can. Their presence in the usual teaching situation makes it difficult for the teacher to function in a way that is helpful to any or gratifying to herself. The hallmark of those who need this special planning is the degree to which "impulse control" has not developed.

I would suggest some experiments in educational function and structure based on the following five psychoanalytic theoretical propositions:

1. Psychic development, like biological maturation, appears to have an intrinsic motor force of its own. Anna Freud (1965a) has called this the child's need to complete development. This can be noted in analytic counseling of parents, where by holding a few things constant, the developmental momentum can be counted on to carry an oedipal child into latency rather than into the distorting prolongation of the oedipal phase. Just as development can be impeded (Provence and Lipton, 1962; Spitz, 1945, 1946, 1959), there are biological and psychological elements which maintain or give fresh impetus to the momentum of development. Biological factors can be seen to contribute to this process in adolescence. All psychological impetus comes from the vicissitudes of the individual's genetic history of object relations. Significant people are necessary to bring about the appearance and development of psychic functions and can be called "organizers" in an analogue to biogenetic development.

2. The astonishing interaction of innumerable and complicated relationships, events, states, and affects causes development to occur in a hierarchical and spiral fashion. An achieved developmental phase not only sets the stage for further development but also may act as the organizer or stimulus for further development. For example, in such a hierarchy, an ego function such as "self-awareness" (Freud, 1914; Hartmann and Loewenstein, 1962; Jacobson, 1964; Lustman, 1966) not only is a precursor but stimulates self-regulation and organization. This may

be a crucial inducer to superego development in the child capable of entering and resolving the oedipal phase.

3. Following a thought of Ernst Kris, crises—after the fashion of phase-specific crises—may also serve as points of organization and stimulus for development. Whether they become the nidus for arrests and fixations or progression may depend on the quantitative factor and accordingly is related to the theory of trauma. Internal discomfort must reach an *intense, but optimal* height to force the child to progressive resolution without the sequelae of either no resolution or the regression and fixation of extreme trauma.

4. For the purpose of certain kinds of research, many aspects of psychoanalytic human development may be conceptualized in learning theory terms. As a limited learning theory this differs dramatically from existing learning theories of academic psychology. Although many differences exist, the primary one is that it occurs within the context of intense object relationships and is not particularly related to such concepts as "reinforcement" or "gratification." It is a learning theory addressed to character development, not to academic content. The key modes of "learning" are the internalization processes.

5. Viewed from the point of view of the structural theory, a complex psychic function, such as internalized impulse control, is itself a *superordinate structure* involving a hierarchical stratification of drive derivatives, defenses, with both ego and superego elements intertwined on ever higher levels of organization. What we call the synthetic function of the ego is usually credited with this task. It may well be that the hierarchy itself is the cohesive and organizing element. Impulse control does not become structuralized definitively until the superego does—from which time internalized moral codes (whatever their cultural content) participate in control. Cognition alone (primarily an ego function) must rely on superego elements to effect this inner state. Otherwise control remains external in the form of the teacher, the cops, etc.

All of these propositions point to the hypothesis that prolonged and intense object ties with one teacher may act as inducer and organizer of psychic function. Once started, the developmental process may get some continuity by virtue of its own force and momentum. The continued and intense relationship may maintain further development by its relationship to crises and their organizational and inducer potentiality. The development of impulse control is the target set of functions by which to select children who need this kind of special educational experience—and is the set of functions by which it can be assessed.

Based on these propositions, I suggest the experiment of assigning *one* (specially selected, specially trained and supported) teacher to a small, nongraded group of impulse-ridden, culturally deprived children. This primary relationship should be of a long enough duration—perhaps eight years—to insure object constancy and unbroken continuity for the child.

The teacher should have genuine, prolonged responsibility for her children. She should teach all content to them, although enrichment can be introduced as usable by the children. The "curriculum" should shift from its focus on content to a primary focus on human object ties. Affection, stimulation, and *absolute, unbroken continuity* are deemed crucial for such an experiment in safeguarding the best interests of the child. It is hoped that within such a setting, developmental impetus can be induced in these deprived children.

It is of interest that such a modification would fit into what two leading educators (Fantini and Weinstein, 1967, 1968) call a "contact curriculum." In their terms the modifications call for the curriculum to be flexibly geared to unique needs of individual schools; that it move from a symbolic (academic) base to an experiential base; that experientially it be immediate in its orientation (rather than past or future); that it shift to social participation (doing) rather than academic participation (knowing); that it explore reality; and that the emphasis move from a sole concern with cognitive content to an "equal emphasis on affective, inner content" (1968; p. 50).

In this troubled era, I must close by repeating that while focusing on education, I am in no sense suggesting exclusion of the existing families, however disorganized. Quite the contrary is indicated— with vigorous social, political, and economic efforts to aid adults. More than that—vigorous research efforts are needed to develop psychological aids to this population.

I have been almost exclusively concerned with ways of making maximal use of the teacher as a *crucial object* in the lives of children. This is with the hope of offsetting the unfortunate circumstances which deprived them of human object ties necessary for development. It is with the hope of setting into motion developmental forces and maintaining developmental momentum. Frequent change of teacher, introduction to a bewildering number of specialty teachers will not enhance the possibility of intense relatedness, which psychoanalytic experience insists is the single most important variable in this problem.

REFERENCES

AICHHORN, A. 1925. *Wayward Youth.* New York: Viking Press, 1935.

BERNFELD, S. 1925. *The Psychology of the Infant.* New York: Brentano, 1929.

BORN, M. 1968. *My Life and My Views.* New York: Scribner.

CHOMSKY, N. 1959. A Review of B. F. Skinner's "Verbal Behavior." *Language,* 35:26–56.

EKSTEIN, R. 1969. Psychoanalytic Notes on the Function of the Curriculum. In: Ekstein and Motto, pp. 47–57.

EKSTEIN, R., AND MOTTO, R. 1969. *From Learning for Love to Love of Learning.* New York: Brunner Mazel.

FANTINI, M., AND WEINSTEIN, G. 1967. Taking Advantage of the Disadvantaged. *The Record: Columbia University,* 69:1–12.

———. 1968. *The Disadvantaged: Challenge to Education.* New York: Harper & Row.

———. 1969. *Toward a Contact Curriculum.* New York: Anti-Defamation League of B'nai B'rith.

FREUD, A. 1931. Introduction to: *Psycho-Analysis for Teachers.* London: Allen & Unwin.

———. 1946. Freedom from Want in Early Education. *The Writings of Anna Freud,* 4:425–441. New York: International Universities Press, 1968.

———. 1954. Psychoanalysis and Education. *The Psychoanalytic Study of the Child,* 9:9–15.

———. 1965a. *Normality and Pathology in Childhood.* New York: International Universities Press.

———. 1965b. Three Contributions to a Seminar on Family Law. *The Writings of Anna Freud,* 5:436–459. New York: International Universities Press, 1969.

FREUD, A., AND BURLINGHAM, D. 1943. *Infants Without Families.* New York: International Universities Press, 1944.

FREUD, S. 1900. The Interpretation of Dreams. *Standard Edition,* 4 & 5. London: Hogarth Press, 1953.

———. 1914. On Narcissism. *Standard Edition,* 14:67–102. London: Hogarth Press, 1957.

GILL, M. M. 1964. *Topography and Systems in Psychoanalytic Theory* [*Psychological Issues,* Monogr. 10]. New York: International Universities Press.

GREENACRE, P. 1945. Conscience in the Psychopath. *Amer. J. Orthopsychiat.*, 15:495–509.

HARTMANN, H. 1947. On Rational and Irrational Action. *Essays on Ego Psychology*. New York: International Universities Press, 1964, pp. 37–68.

———. 1955. Notes on the Theory of Sublimation. *Essays on Ego Psychology*. New York: International Universities Press, 1964, pp. 215–240.

———. 1960. *Psychoanalysis and Moral Values*. New York: International Universities Press.

HARTMANN, H., AND LOEWENSTEIN, R. M. 1962. Notes on the Superego. *This Annual*, 17:42–81.

JACOBSON, E. 1964. *The Self and the Object World*. New York: International Universities Press.

KOESTLER, A. 1967. *The Ghost in the Machine*. New York: Macmillan.

KRIS, E. 1948. On Psychoanalysis and Education. *Amer. J. Orthopsychiat.*, 18:622–635.

LUSTMAN, S. L. 1966. Impulse Control, Structure, and the Synthetic Function. In: *Psychoanalysis—A General Psychology*, ed. R. M. Loewenstein, L. M. Newman, M. Schur, & A. J. Solnit. New York: International Universities Press, pp. 190–221.

MAHLER, M. S. 1963. Thoughts about Development and Individuation. *The Psychoanalytic Study of the Child,* 18:307–324.

OMWAKE, E. 1966. The Child's Estate. In: *Modern Perspectives in Child Development,* ed. A. J. Solnit & S. Provence. New York: International Universities Press, pp. 577–594.

PELLER, L. 1946. Incentives to Development and Means of Early Education. *The Psychoanalytic Study of the Child,* 2:397–415.

———. 1956. The School's Role in Promoting Sublimation. *The Psychoanalytic Study of the Child,* 11:437–449.

Piaget, J. 1923. *The Language and Thought of the Child*. London; Routledge, 1932.

———. 1932. *The Moral Judgment of the Child*. Glencoe, Ill.: Free Press, 1948.

PIERS, G., AND PIERS, M. 1965. Modes of Learning and the Analytic Process. *Selected Lectures: Sixth International Congress of Psychotherapy*. London, New York: S. Karger.

PROVENCE, S., AND LIPTON, R. C. 1962. *Infants in Institutions*. New York: International Universities Press.

SIMPSON, G. G. 1967. The Crisis in Biology. *Amer. Scholar*, 36:363–377.

Skinner, B. F. 1957. *Verbal Behavior*. New York: Macmillan.

Spitz, R. A. 1945. Hospitalism. *The Psychoanalytic Study of the Child,* 1:53–74.

———. 1946. Hospitalism: A Follow-up Report. *The Psychoanalytic Study of the Child,* 2:113–117.

————. 1959. *A Genetic Field Theory of Ego Formation.* New York: International Universities Press.

VON BERTALANFFY, L. 1967. *Robots, Men and Minds.* New York: Braziller.

WAELDER, R. 1930. The Principle of Multiple Function. *Psa. Quart.*, 5:45–62, 1936.

AFTERWORD

You have read a variety of different kinds of articles dealing with the effects of the cultural environment on the developing human being. What relevance does this information have for you personally? We obviously cannot answer that question for you, since each one of you will, based on your own past experience and interests, have selected and filtered different information from all that you have read as having particular interest to you. For example, if you are an expectant parent, you may have been interested in the concept of an exterogestation period and its implications for your practice as a parent in those first nine months after birth. No doubt, your thinking was also stimulated by the articles discussing the influences of their emotional environment on children's physical and mental growth. If you are in the medical or allied professions, you might have been fascinated by the descriptions of the children in the articles on dwarfism; if you are not, you probably skimmed over that terminology, since it likely had no meaning to you personally.

Whatever your particular interest, however, *as a human being,* there are several aspects of the volume that should provoke you to think about your own personal responsibilities to the continued growth and development of humanity. First, on an individual level, for those of you who are now or plan to be parents, the information presented should serve to alert you to just how important your influence on your children's growth and development really is. Many recent books on childrearing assert that too much attention was paid in the past to children's social and emotional development at the expense of their intellectual development. We question whether enough *informed* attention has really ever been paid to the development of children with healthy self-concepts, who are able to grow up with good feelings about themselves as well as the ability to get along well with others. Be that as it may, we are concerned with the over-attention by some writers to children's intellectual development at the expense (or at least the neglect) of their social and emotional development. Dr. Montagu has presented eloquent and dramatic testimony to the possible effects of the emotional environment on the growing child. This information should at least cause you to question an over-intellectualized approach to childrearing and to realize the devastating influence emotional conditions can have on children's total development.

Second, on a social level, we must all, as human beings, ask whether our attitudes and practices toward others of other ethnic origins in any way prohibits their full growth as human beings. Regardless of any differences that may exist between different populations, we are all more alike than we are different. We share a common humanity, and any inhibition of growth and development of any group is ultimately at the expense of all humanity. The important questions are not what the average IQ score of any population is, or how many creative and productive individuals have emerged from its ranks, but rather, what opportunity its members have had to *fully* actualize whatever potential they have, not as a group, but as individuals. If you have to worry about eating and safety, you are not in a position to express your full potential as a human being.

It is much too late to continue blaming the less fortunate sectors of our society and of the world for the condition they are in. We all, as human beings, have a responsibility for one another, and those who are in positions of power and influence have an obligation to work toward the equalization of opportunity (in the sense that Dr. Montagu discusses it) of all peoples. At the very least, each individual must examine his own patterns of behavior to make sure that he is not where he is at the expense of other, less fortunate people.

There is one rule of human interaction that we must readopt if we are to survive as a species. It is one that has shown up in some form in almost every human culture that has ever existed, and it embodies the two important elements of human development: individuality *and* cooperation. You may do what you will as long as it is not (directly or indirectly) at the expense of another. If we all work toward behavior that reflects a concern for this rule, we may all become human and humane again.

J. L. B.
L. D. B.

RESOURCES

ASKIN, JOHN A., COOKE, ROBERT E., AND HALLER, JR., J. ALEX, EDS. *A Symposium on the Child*. Baltimore: Johns Hopkins University Press, 1967.

BARNOUW, VICTOR. *Culture and Personality*. Homewood, Illinois: Dorsey Press, 1963.

HOFFMAN, LOIS WLADIS, AND HOFFMAN, MARTIN L. *Review of Child Development Research*, 3 vols. New York: Russell Sage Foundation, 1964, 1966, 1972.

HUDSON, LIAM, ED. *The Ecology of Human Intelligence*. Baltimore: Penguin Books, 1970.

HUNT, J. McV. *Intelligence and Experience*. New York: Ronald Press, 1961.

MONEY, JOHN, AND EHRHARDT, ANKE A. *Man & Woman, Boy & Girl*. Baltimore: Johns Hopkins University Press, 1972.

MONTAGU, ASHLEY. *The Human Revolution*. New York: Bantam Books, 1967.

———. *On Being Human*, rev. ed. New York: Hawthorn Books, 1966.

———. *The Direction of Human Development*, rev. ed. New York: Hawthorn Books, 1970.

MUSSEN, PAUL H., ED. *Carmichael's Manual of Child Psychology*, 2 vols. New York: John Wiley, 1970.

PATTON, ROBERT GRAY, AND GARDNER, LYTT I. *Growth Failure in Maternal Deprivation*. Springfield, Illinois: Charles C Thomas, 1963.

SANDERS, BARKEV S. *Environment and Growth*. Baltimore: Warwick & York, 1934.

WATSON, E. H. AND G. H. LOWREY, *Growth and Development of Children*, 5th ed. Chicago: Yearbook Medical Publishers, 1967.

NEBRASKA WESTERN COLLEGE
LIBRARY